Lake's Campaigns
in India

Lake's Campaign's in India

The Second Anglo-Maratha War
1803–1807

Hugh Pearse

LEONAUR

Lake's Campaigns in India: the Second Anglo Maratha War, 1803-1807
by Hugh Pearse

Adapted by the Leonaur editors from the 1908 volume
*Memoir of the Life and Military Services of Viscount Lake,
Baron Lake of Delhi and Laswaree 1744-1808*

Published by Leonaur Ltd

ISBN: 978-1-84677-253-5 (hardcover)
ISBN: 978-1-84677-254-2 (softcover)

http://www.leonaur.com

Publisher's Note

The opinions expressed in this book are those of the author
and are not necessarily those of the publisher.

Contents

Introduction

Gerard Lake (July 27, 1744—February 20, 1808) entered the Foot Guards in 1758, and was promoted to lieutenant in 1762. He achieved a captaincy in 1776, majority 1784, and became lieutenant colonel in 1792, by which time he was a general officer in the army. He served with the guards in Germany, in 1760-1762, and with a composite battalion at the Battle of Yorktown of 1781 in the final stages of the American war of independence. After returning to Britain he was equerry to the Prince of Wales, afterwards George IV. In 1790 he became a major-general, and in 1793 was appointed to command the Guards Brigade in the Duke of York's army in Flanders during the Napoleonic Wars. He was in command at the brilliant action of Lincelles, on 18 August 1793, and served in Europe (except for a short time during a period of illness) until April 1794. He had now sold his lieutenant-colonelcy in the Guards and became colonel of the 53rd foot and governor of Limerick, Ireland. In 1797 he was promoted lieutenant-general.

The following year—1798—the Irish rebellion broke out. Lake, who was in the country, succeeded Sir Ralph Abercromby in command of the army in April 1798, issued a proclamation ordering the surrender of all arms by the civil population of Ulster. Commanding some 20,000 troops he suppressed the Wexford rebels and defeated the main rebel army at Vinegar Hill (near Enniscorthy, County Wexford on 21st June. In August Lake opposed a French expedition of 1,000 troops which had landed at Killala Bay, County Mayo on 23rd August. On the 29th of the same month Lake arrived at Castlebar with a force of 6,000 troops, only to witness the rout of his troops under General Hely-Hutchinson and the loss of his baggage. He finally retrieved the situation forcing the surrender of the French at Ballinamuck on 8th September 1798.

After the suppression of the Irish rebellion of Lake remained for some time in Ireland, and entered the Irish Parliament as member for Armagh, voting, as a matter of course, for the Union. In October 1800 his services were rewarded with the great appointment of Commander-in-Chief in India, for which country he presently sailed, arriving at Calcutta on January 31, 1801.

Lake was accompanied by his second son, Captain George Lake, 34th Regiment, as aide-de-camp, and also by his four unmarried daughters.

His appointment to this great independent command gave him the opportunity of showing that he had mastered the secret of success in war, the one rule to which there is no exception, the superiority of activity over inaction, of the attack over the defence. Such a line of conduct was no doubt natural to Lake from his inborn character, and all the events of his long military career had confirmed him in the belief that the course which was natural to him was also the best. In early youth he had borne a part in the operations of the great Frederick, though not under his immediate command; in America he had shared in the humiliation of Yorktown, when Cornwallis, even if by no fault of his own, took up the role of passive defence; at Lincelles his weak brigade had triumphed over a largely superior force strongly posted; and in Ireland he had witnessed a similar triumph won by a French column of much the same strength and composition. Everywhere he had seen the attack triumph, the defensive fail. From such a lifelong experience we may imagine how a belief grew in the mind of Lake that to the bold all things were possible; and now, at the age of fifty-six, he was enabled to put his theory into practice; and, as will be seen, he did so in the most consistent manner, and with a success that has been rarely equalled in war.

CHAPTER 1

The Maratha War—1803

The Maratha power was founded in the middle of the seventeenth century by Sivaji, who formed a state in the south-western portion of the moribund Moghul empire. It tended to decay under his son Sambaji, was restored by two great officers, Mulharji Holkar and Ranoji Sindhia, but was for a time crushed by the defeat of its armies at Panipat in 1761 by the Afghan invader Ahmad Shah Abdali.

From Panipat there escaped one of the house of Sindhia, Madhaji by name, who by his extraordinary talents restored his race to its former power and influence. Ten years after the battle of Panipat, Madhaji Sindhia entered Delhi as a conqueror, the titular emperor, Shah Alam, in his train. In 1778 he came to blows with the English, and owing to the feebleness and incompetence of the Bombay Government, forced on it the humiliating treaty of Wargaum in 1779. This treaty was repudiated by Warren Hastings, the Governor-General, who sent a small force across India, from east to west, and retrieved the reputation lost in Bombay. In 1780 Madhaji was defeated by Camac in Central India, and his most valued possession, the great fortress of Gwalior, was captured by a small detachment under Major Popham—an astonishing exploit. Warren Hastings, while thus checking the Marathas, was conducting a desperate war in the south of India against

Haidar Ali of Mysore, who was supported by France. He was therefore willing to come to terms with the Marathas, and peace with them was concluded in February 1782.

Thus set free, Madhaji Sindhia soon became paramount in Western, Central, and North-Western India, obtaining for the Peshwa, who, though a Brahman, was nominally the head of the Marathas, the title of Vice Regent of the Empire, but himself ruling as the deputy of the Peshwa and of the Emperor. Realising that he who desired to be supreme in India must sooner or later measure his strength with the British, Sindhia next set about the reorganisation of an army on the European model, under the command of some 300 officers of various nationalities, but chiefly French.

Death now intervened, and just as Madhaji Sindhia was preparing a general combination against the English, he died of fever in February 1794. Madhaji was succeeded by his great-nephew, Daolat Rao Sindhia, whose youth stood against his claim to preponderance, and once more the Maratha states were at variance one with the other.

It may be convenient, at this point, to explain the geographical terms used in India in 1803. Hindustan was the name then, and indeed still, applied by the natives to the tract of country south of the Punjab, and lying between the rivers Sutlej and Chambal. In its easterly portion were included the provinces of Oudh and Rohilkhand. South of the Chambal lay Rajputana, and east of that country were the states of Malwa and Gwalior, the original possessions of Sindhia and Holkar. Yet farther east lay Bhopal and Bundelkhand. South of the Narbada was the region known as the "Deccan" (or southland), itself divided into many kingdoms and lesser states.

Lord Wellesley, then Lord Mornington, arrived in India in April 1798 with instructions to preserve the balance of power between the native princes as provided by the treaty of Seringapatam (1792). The dissensions among the

Maratha states had already altered the balance, and their consequent weakness had conferred a dangerous strength on Tipu of Mysore, the successor of Haidar, who was arranging an alliance with the French and encouraging an Afghan invasion of Northern India. Lord Mornington was consequently compelled to declare war against Tipu, who was defeated and killed at Seringapatam in April 1799. Lord Mornington was created an Irish marquis, and thenceforth appears in history under his new title of Wellesley.

During and after the Mysore War the struggle for the mastery between the leading Maratha chiefs continued to grow in intensity, and year by year the difficulty of preserving the peace in India grew greater. A further complication had been caused by the death in 1795 of Tukaji Rao Holkar, the ruler of Indore, and the consequent struggle among his sons for the reversion of his power. Finally, Jaswant Rao, the ablest among them, seized the throne of Indore, and immediately entered on a war with Sindhia. The unfortunate Peshwa, the nominal head of the Maratha princes, fell under the sway of Holkar and Sindhia alternately, as one or the other triumphed. In October 1802 Holkar defeated the forces of the Peshwa and of Sindhia before Poona, the Maratha capital; but this victory had a disastrous effect on Holkar's fortunes, and brought matters to a climax, for the Peshwa now fled from both Sindhia and Holkar and placed himself under British protection, signing on the last day of 1802 the treaty of Bassein.

It was obvious that this treaty, which made the head of the Maratha confederacy a permanent tributary of the British Government, would be a severe blow to Holkar and Sindhia, who both aspired in the future to control the Peshwa, and Lord Wellesley, while far from desirous of war, and while showing the utmost patience towards the angry chieftains, was compelled to prepare to meet an attack.

The first essential was to protect the Peshwa from being dragged into war against his will, and with this object the Governor-General directed his brother, Major-General Arthur Wellesley, to march on Poona from Mysore with 15,000 troops. Holkar was still in occupation of the Maratha capital; but he had not yet come to terms with Sindhia or the Raja of Berar, the other leading Maratha chief of the south, and he was not minded to fight the British single-handed. He therefore fell back into his own dominions as General Wellesley approached, and the latter occupied Poona without firing a shot on April 20, 1803.

At the same time that Lord Wellesley ordered his brother to advance on Poona, he sent orders to General Lake, who was at Cawnpore, to be in readiness to commence hostilities against Sindhia in the north at any moment.

The question of peace or war now rested with Sindhia, to whom the unpalatable fact was evident that if he acquiesced in the treaty of Bassein he would never realise the Maratha Empire designed by his great-uncle, nor the expulsion of the English from India. The patience shown by Lord Wellesley in giving Sindhia ample time to make up his mind was even excelled by Colonel Collins, the Resident at Sindhia's Court, who was most anxious to avert war. Negotiations dragged on until the month of June, when Sindhia and the Berar Raja had prolonged interviews, Colonel Collins repeatedly pressing Sindhia to declare his intentions. No answer was obtainable, and it soon became evident that the two chiefs were endeavouring to persuade Holkar to join them.

At last, about the middle of July, the tension became unendurable, and Lord Wellesley directed his brother to call on Sindhia and the Berar Raja to separate their armies, adding that if Sindhia would return to his own dominions the British troops would also retire into their cantonments.

To this appeal no definite answer was given, and the Maratha armies remained united.

Lord Wellesley having waited from June 4, the date on which the two Maratha chieftains had their first meeting, to August 1, saw that Sindhia and the Bhonsla intended war though they would not declare it, directed Colonel Collins to leave Sindhia's camp, and ordered the armies of Lake and Arthur Wellesley to commence operations.

The total strength of regular troops in the three presidencies on the outbreak of the Maratha War was approximately as follows:[1]

British cavalry	2,880
British infantry	14,500
Native cavalry	5,850
Native infantry	81,480

Or a total of 104,710 cavalry and infantry, with 2,400 artillerymen.

The only Horse Artillery battery in India was in process of formation, and was not fit for service until the war had been some time in progress. The bulk of the artillery was distributed among units, two light, or galloper, guns being attached to each cavalry regiment, while each brigade of infantry also had with it a proportion of guns.

It need hardly be stated that the Anglo-Indian army was widely scattered, and it was only by running very considerable risks that Lord Wellesley was able to put about 60,000 men into the field.

It is very difficult to ascertain the real strength of the armies of Sindhia and the Berar Raja. According to Thorn, who was supplied with information by English officers who had recently left the Maratha service, Sindhia had about 40,000 regular troops, with 450 guns, in addition to

---

1. *The Campaigns of Lord Lake Against the Marathas.* Major Helsham Jones, R.E. 1881.

an immense number of irregulars. His artillery was much superior in training and in *matériel* to that of any army previously encountered by the British in India; and his regular infantry, though written of in these pages, as in other works, as Marathas, were in fact almost to a man natives of Oudh, Rohilkhand, and the Doab.

The Berar Raja's army, though inferior in training to that of Sindhia, was formidable from its numbers, had a powerful artillery and contained an Arab contingent of excellent fighting quality. According to Grant-Duff, and there is no higher authority, the united armies of Sindhia and the Berar Raja totalled about 100,000 men, of whom 50,000 were horse, and upwards of 30,000 were regular infantry and artillery. In addition were from 10,000 to 12,000 men under a chief named Shamshir Bahadur, who held Bundelkhand as a tributary of the Peshwa, and joined the confederacy: against the British.

As we are concerned with the operations of General Lake's army only, a mere sketch will now be given of the general plan of campaign which had been decided on by General Lake's consultation with the Governor-General and Major-General Arthur Wellesley.

The circumstances leading up to the declaration of war had caused a concentration of troops in the neighbourhood of Poona. These troops were divided into two corps,—one commanded by Major-General Arthur Wellesley, the other by Colonel Stevenson, who, however, acted under Wellesley's orders. Attached to the combined force were some Mysore cavalry and a mounted corps contributed by the Peshwa. Altogether, General Wellesley had (about 17,000 men under his orders, of whom 5,000 were auxiliaries of poor quality. He had also a reserve of 7,000 men close at hand. General Wellesley's task was to destroy the armies of Sindhia and the Raja of Berar, who together had in the southern theatre of war about 50,000 men, with upwards of 100 guns.

The Maratha states in 1803 ran right across India, the province of Cuttack, which belonged to Berar, lying on the north-east coast of the peninsula and dividing the Bengal and Madras presidencies. On the west the Gaikwar's dominions in Gujarat had a long sea-board to the north-west of Bombay. The Gaikwar, the chief of the western Marathas, whose capital at this time was Ahmadabad, had not joined in the war, but his attitude was uncertain.

Two forces were therefore allotted to the two maritime states, 5,000 men under Colonel Harcourt having instructions to seize Cuttack, while 4,200 men under Colonel Woodington were to occupy Gujarat. To dispose of the minor operations, it may suffice to say that both Colonels Harcourt and Woodington achieved their objects with ease, and the Marathas were consequently cut off from any hope of assistance by sea from the French.

In the northern theatre of war General Lake himself commanded. Under his personal orders was a force which when concentrated amounted to about 10,000 men. This force, immediately before the outbreak of war, lay in its cantonments at Cawnpore, Fatehgarh, and some smaller stations in the ceded districts of Oudh.

General Lake also had at his orders a force of 8,500 men stationed at Allahabad, under Lieut.-Colonel Powell. This force was intended to deal with Shamshir Bahadur and occupy the province of Bundelkhand as soon as Lake considered it safe for it to advance.

The share to be taken by the Commander-in-Chief in the widely extended operations which he had planned with Lord Wellesley was to be no light one. He had undertaken, with his very small force, to deal first with that portion of, the disciplined army created for Sindhia by Count de Boigne and General Perron that might be found in the region styled by Lord Wellesley "the French state." This term referred to the *Doab*, the great territory lying between the rivers Ganges and Jumna which had been handed over successively to the two French generals for the payment and equipment of the regular army, and to provide their own salaries. De Boigne had left India in 1795, and the command had since been exercised by General Perron, who was now not only commander-in-chief of Sindhia's army, but had recently been practically dictator of the dominions of the King of Delhi and wielder of the power that still attached to the government of the Moghul empire. In support of this army—formidable enough by itself from its numerical strength, training, and discipline—were the vast hordes of irregulars of various nationalities that served Sindhia himself and the numerous princes of Hindustan, all more likely to support the actual master of Delhi than the numerically weak British army. Behind them again were the Sikhs and Afghans, unlikely, it is true, to act in unison with one another, but either power a source of danger in the event of a reverse to Lake's small force.

As regards the strength of Sindhia's army in Hindustan, the greater part of the regular battalions were, shortly before the war, far away in the Deccan, but Perron himself had remained in the north and had nineteen battalions with him. Fifteen more had been ordered up from Sindhia's own territory to Delhi, and were rapidly approaching. Perron's force, well armed and equipped, was based on the strongly fortified cities of Delhi and Agra, which were provided with independent garrisons, and on his arsenal in the great fortress of Aligarh. The Maratha regular army had in the past often shown high fighting quality, and was composed of veteran soldiers drawn from the fighting races of Hindustan, inured to the hardships of war and accustomed to victory.

To meet this fine force in the field, and to capture its

strong places, Lake had no more at his disposal than 10,000 men of all arms; and inasmuch as it seemed to him more important to strike his first blow before his enemy expected him to move, than to await the concentration of the whole of his small army, he actually took the field with little more than half this in considerable force.

In addition to the destruction of Sindhia's regular army in Hindustan and the capture of his strongholds, Lake undertook with his meagre 10,000 to defend the northern and western frontiers of Bengal against the operations of Sindhia, devoting to that duty two of his three brigades of cavalry and one brigade of infantry, which watched the frontier near Cawnpore during the opening stages of the campaign.

It appears in the correspondence between Lake and Lord Wellesley prior to outbreak of war that there was a difference of opinion between them as to the safer course of action for the former to pursue. Lord Wellesley suggested the capture of Delhi and Agra as the first steps, Perron's army and Aligarh to be dealt with subsequently. General Lake, with all the deference to the Governor-General suggested by his strong sense of discipline, held firmly to his own view, that no movement on Delhi would be safe with Aligarh and Perron's regular army left between himself and his base at Allahabad. Lake admitted the risk, pointed out by Lord Wellesley, that while he was attacking Aligarh, Sindhia might slip past him and raid the Company's territory, but he maintained that his plan of campaign was the less dangerous of the two.

The Governor-General, who was superior to all false pride, frankly gave way, and it is hard to say which of the disputants deserves the higher honour. Lord Wellesley was unaccustomed to encounter such independence of character, and that he valued it appears from the tone of his correspondence with Lake. Courteous from the first, it soon abounded in expressions of cordial friendship as the course of the campaign and its vicissitudes made him fully acquainted with the courageous and generous character of Lake. Generosity and courage indeed were congenial qualities to Lord Wellesley, who, like Lake, was ever ready to assume responsibility or to shield a subordinate.

In addition to the military programme which he himself had laid down, entailing the capture of Aligarh, the destruction of Perron's regular troops, and the occupation or capture of Delhi and Agra, Lake had committed to him the task of imposing British protection on Shah Alam, the Moghul emperor or King of Delhi, and of establishing a resident political officer at his Court. For this purpose, and to enable him to make treaties of alliance with such princes of the Rajput and other races in the theatre of war as he might be able to detach from the Maratha cause, Lake was entrusted by Lord Wellesley with full political powers.

We must now glance at the composition and organisation of the 10,000 troops with which Lake had undertaken his formidable and complex task, nearly half the strength of which was at first employed to hold Sindhia in check and to guard the British frontier from invasion.

The composition of Lake's 10,000 was as follows: 8 regiments of cavalry, forming 3 brigades; 13 battalions of infantry, forming 4 brigades.

The only European infantry regiment was the 76th, which was placed in the 1st Brigade, and took the right of the line in action.

The artillery, commanded by Lieut.-Colonel John Horsford, consisting of 32 guns and howitzers. Of these, 16 guns were allotted as galloper guns to the cavalry—i.e., 2 to each regiment. The remainder were divided among the infantry brigades as shown in the distribution statement.

The cavalry brigades had each two staff officers—a major of brigade and a brigade quartermaster. Colonel St Leger, the senior Brigadier, commanded all the cavalry, but had no additional staff for this duty.

In practice, General Lake himself took command of the cavalry as soon as it came into action, joining the infantry when the turn of that arm for active work came about.

The infantry, with a staff on no larger scale than that of the cavalry, was divided into wings. The right wing, composed of the 1st and 3rd Brigades, was commanded by Major-General Robert Ware, a veteran officer of the Company's service; and the left, composed of the 2nd and 4th Brigades, by Major-General the Hon. Frederick St John, an officer, young for his position, zealous, active, and capable of original thought.

The distribution of the regiments of cavalry and infantry into brigades was as under:

CAVALRY

	Commanders
1st Brigade	Colonel T. P. Vandeleur
H.M.'s 8th Light Dragoons	Lieut.-Col. J. Vandeleur
1st Bengal Cavalry	Lieut.-Col. Gordon
3rd Bengal Cavalry	Major Middleton
2nd Brigade	Colonel St Leger
H.M.'s 27th Light Dragoons	Lieut.-Colonel Need
2nd Bengal Cavalry	Lieut.-Colonel Brown
6th Bengal Cavalry	Major Mounsey
3rd Brigade	Colonel R. Macan
H.M.'s 29th Light Dragoons	Lieut.-Col. C. Carleton
Bengal Cavalry	Lieut.-Col. M'Gregor

INFANTRY

1st Brigade	Colonel W. Monson

Lake's force was a very small one for the task in hand, and notably weak in artillery, though in Lieut.-Colonel Horsford that arm had a highly able and experienced commander. The force, however, had been highly trained for war by

Lake himself, and some description of the circumstances in which it had received this training may be interesting, and will also serve to explain the complete mutual confidence which existed between the General and his small army.

From the moment of General Lake's arrival in India, it had been evident to Lord Wellesley that war with the Marathas might suddenly be forced upon him; and the Governor-General had therefore directed Lake to make his headquarters at Cawnpore, instead of Calcutta. This arrangement, in those days of slow postal communication, had its drawbacks, but the result had been an exceptional war training of the Bengal army during the cold weather of 1802. Cawnpore was then garrisoned by British troops in accordance with a treaty with the Nawab-Wazir of Oudh, and at no great distance lay a great tract of open country, round the vast ruins of the ancient city of Kanauj. In this terrain, General Lake supervised the training for war of all the available regiments of British and native cavalry in Bengal. The training had been carried out by Colonel St Leger, but the system was Lake's own invention, special attention being paid to a novel use of "galloper" or horse-artillery guns. Two of these guns were attached to each regiment, and "nothing," writes Captain Thorn, who was present as a staff officer of cavalry, "could exceed the celerity and exactness of the manoeuvres made with them at full speed by this large body of cavalry, whose combined movements, conducted with the most perfect order, and in a spirit of emulation, gave certain promise of the glory which, in the space of a few months, afterwards crowned their labours."

Such continuous training gave Lake an opportunity, rare in those days, of testing the capabilities of his officers and men, who in turn learned to know what their General expected of them, and imbibed much of his fearless and confident spirit.

Nor did the association of Lake with his officers end on parade. Kanauj was then a happy hunting-ground, for, writes Thorn, "here amidst lofty grass, covering the ruins of splendid edifices and the tombs of princes, lay concealed a variety of game; while beasts of prey, such as wolves, jackals, and tigers, secluded them-selves in retreats which formerly had resounded with the voice of gladness. On one of these hunting excursions a tiger of large size was shot with a pistol by General Lake, just as the ferocious animal was in the act of springing upon Major Nairne, by whom it had been previously speared."

This was indeed hunting in the fearless old fashion, and carried on, doubtless, in full uniform. Major Nairne, a well-known *shikari* of the period, was, it may be added, killed in action very shortly afterwards, during the operations carried on by General Lake against certain insurgent Zemindars in the ceded districts.

The training at the camp of exercise at Kanauj in the cold weather of 1802-3 was perhaps the first on a large scale experienced by any portion of the Anglo-Indian army, and the Spartan soldiers of to-day may be amused by the enthusiastic Captain Thorn's account of the manner in which General Lake allowed his officers to temper hard and useful work with convivial and even domestic pleasures. Lake's four beautiful daughters accompanied him into camp, and aided him in dispensing the lavish hospitality in which he delighted. "Military occupations," says Thorn, "were diversified with the scenes of social harmony and festivity. . . . The heat of the day was moderate, but the nights were cold; and many officers had not only glass doors to their tents, but chimneys of bricks, by which means they were enabled to enjoy the pleasures of an English fireside with their wives and families, who had been allowed to accompany them on this occasion. These domestic comforts were heightened by the luxuries of the table, where were the finest wines of every kind, from the exhilarating *sheeraz* of Persia to the ruby carbonelle and humble port." Those were hardy days, and when we find the port of our grand-sires described as "humble," and taking the lowest place in the descending scale of the worthy chronicler's list of Kanauj beverages, we tremble to think how exhilarating must have been the "sheeraz of Persia."

While thus gaining the affection of his officers, whom he entertained with lavish hospitality and with the dignified geniality for which he was famed in his day, General Lake succeeded in endearing himself no less to the rank and file of his cavalry. The hardy and daring-Light Dragoons of the royal service saw at their head a leader after their own heart, for, although in his fifty-ninth year, Lake headed every charge in manoeuvre as he afterwards did in war; and the cavalry soldier who does not respect and like a hard rider has yet to be found.

In the dignified and courteous Guardsman, too, the self-respecting sowars of the Bengal cavalry, unerring judges of a man, found an ideal "Lord of War"; and the respect now inspired in them by the activity and skill of Lake, or *"Lick sahib bahadur"* as they called him, was soon turned into a warm affection and devotion to the brave veteran, whom they were soon to see riding through their camps in lean days, munching as they did, in the saddle, a handful of parched grain, and declaring it a sufficient diet for the true soldier.

While the cavalry at Kanauj was thus preparing for war while enjoying the pleasures of peace, the infantry regiments cantoned at Cawnpore, Fatehgarh, and other stations in Oudh, were being provided by Major-General St John with an organisation of light infantry companies similar to those introduced about the same time into the army in

England. For this purpose ten men in each company were selected for special training as light infantry and marksmen. These men remained on the strength of their companies, of which there were ten in each battalion, but when required to perform their special functions they were called to the front, and formed an eleventh company. On the line of march they were thrown out by signal to guard the flanks of the column.

General Lake approved of this arrangement as a temporary measure, but preferred the formation of a special native rifle-corps, which was subsequently raised. The objection to General St John's plan was, of course, the serious weakening of the companies (which were about 90 strong) by the removal of so large a proportion of their best men from their ranks at the moment of going into action.

During the hot weather of 1803 the army lay in its cantonments at Cawnpore, Fatehgarh, and elsewhere, and it was not until August 7 that, war being now inevitable, General Lake acted on his full political authority and marched from Cawnpore with the troops stationed there under Major-General St John. The cavalry from the same station marched on the following day, under Colonel St Leger.

Thirteen days later the army, which had been joined on the road by the troops from Fatehgarh under Major-General Ware, arrived on the British frontier at a place about 112 miles distant from its starting-point. The troops were now distributed into their brigades and continued their advance, encamping on August 28 within sight of the mosque—the most prominent building in the then flourishing town of Koil. The movements of the army had been hindered by the annual rains, which had been unusually light, and had now ceased; and the weather, as is ever the case in what is termed "a break of the rains," was now extremely hot and oppressive, and the troops suffered much from thirst.

In other respects they were in good case, for their camp equipment was on a liberal scale; and to prevent fever Lake had taken the precaution of providing every European soldier with a bedstead, one of the strong and light cots used by the natives of India, and known as *charpoys*.

The line of march of an army in India is still an interesting spectacle, but a hundred years ago it was indeed astonishing, resembling rather the migration of a population than that of a mere fighting force. The transport of the East has ever been cumbrous, and was at this period entirely irregular, while the number of camp-followers in Lake's army was estimated at ten persons to every fighting man. A force of 10,000 soldiers, approximately the number now operating in the Doab, would therefore have had 100,000 followers; and their motley nature, and the various descriptions of vehicles and: animals required for the carriage of their habitations and supplies, merit the transcription of Captain Thorn's vivid picture of the march of an Indian army of the olden time.

First stating that several hundred elephant and some thousands of camels were required to carry the camp equipage and their own provender, Thorn writes:

> Every horse, whether of the cavalry or not, has two attendants, one who cleans and takes care of the animal, and another, denominated the grass-cutter, who gathers forage, consisting of the roots of grass, which he digs up with an iron instrument resembling a mason's trowel. These roots, being carefully washed, constitute an excellent food; and in fact no other could well be obtained in a climate which, when the hot wind prevails, is so completely bare of vegetation that not a single blade can be discerned above ground ; not withstanding which dreariness, we have by the means here described been able to preserve all our

cattle when encamped on plains exhibiting nothing but an interminable waste of sterility.

Besides an immense number of draught bullocks for the use of the artillery park and heavy ordnance carts, to every three of which there is at least one driver, large droves of *Brinjarree* bullocks, from eighty to one hundred thousand, are employed in carrying grain. These *Brinjarries*, or more correctly *Bandjarrahs*, are a peculiar class of Hindus, who mix very little with the other tribes. They are a hardy race of people, who live by collecting grain in districts where it is easily procured, and selling it in places where the harvests have been less abundant. Thus they are constantly occupied in travelling to great distances, accompanied by their wives and families; and as they go in large bodies, armed with matchlocks, spears, scimitars, and shields, they can easily stand their ground even against a considerable force. In time of war the Bandjarrahs are of the utmost utility to the party that secures their services, for knowing well where grain is to be obtained, when their stock begins to be exhausted they set out to procure fresh supplies either by purchase or plunder.

To these purveyors of the army, as they may be properly called, who, with their connexions, surpass calculation, must be added in the public department the palankeen and dhoolie bearers, a class of persons at all times necessary in this country, and indispensably so when the fatigues and casualties of war require their assistance for the conveyance of the sick and wounded. An army is further numerically increased by the servants which every officer is under the necessity of employing to take charge of his live and dead stock; for though the private European soldier receives, besides his regular allowance of arrack, rations of meat from the Government contractors, who drive large flocks of sheep for that purpose, the officers must provide their own poultry, sheep, and particularly goats to supply them with milk for their tea—a beverage in this country s of the most refreshing nature, especially after a long march. The attendants, therefore, which these services render expedient, may be estimated at ten to a subaltern, twenty to a captain, thirty to a field officer, and so on in proportion. But even the privates themselves are not without their dependants who contribute to enlarge the population of a camp, there being a cook or *bhabajee* to every mess, a water-carrier or *mesalljee* to each tent, in which lie generally ten or twelve soldiers; also a washer-man, termed a *dhoby*, to every troop or company.

Such are the immediate adjuncts of a inarching force in the East; but even this is pot all, for besides the women who follow the fortunes of the officers and private soldiers, there is a mixed multitude of different denominations termed ' the bazaar people,' consisting of merchants and pedlars, with a variety of adventurers of all pursuits, some exercising particular callings and making themselves useful, while others accompany the army merely with a view to plunder.

Captain Thorn follows up this spirited sketch of the impedimenta of an Indian army by an equally vivid description of the normal formation of Lake's army when on the march and in camp, and of its manner of life when halted, all so unlike the fashion of modern warfare that the reader will perhaps pardon yet another quotation:

The march of our army had the appearance of a moving town or citadel, in the form of an oblong square, whose sides were defended by ramparts of glittering swords and bayonets. On one side moved the line of infantry, on the opposite that of the cavalry, parallel to and preserving its encamping distance as near as possible from the infantry, and keeping the heads of the columns abreast of one another. The front face was protected by the advanced-guard, consisting of all the picquets coming on duty, and the rear by all the picquets returning from duty, and then forming the rear-guard. The parks and columns of artillery moved on in the inside of the square, always keeping the high-road, and next to the infantry, which moved at a short distance from it. The remainder of the space within the square was occupied by the baggage, cattle, and followers of the camp. Notwithstanding the immense magnitude of this moving mass, and the multifarious elements of which it consisted, nothing could exceed the regularity observed by the troops in maintaining their respective distances and adhering closely to the order of formation on the march. The Commander-in-Chief, aware how active the numerous cavalry of the enemy would be in hovering continually round, ready to dart in and take advantage of any opening or improper lengthening out of the line of march, judged it prudent to give the officers a little advice, the excellence of which may recommend it for general adoption no less than for military operations in India. The officers were enjoined to impress upon their men the necessity of acting in perfect concert, without which the advantages of discipline would be lost: they were therefore cautioned, as they regarded their own personal safety and that of the service, not to be led away by a mistaken and reprehensible ardour to break their ranks and so to put themselves on an equality with an irregular and undisciplined enemy.

The army encamped for the most part as it marched—the infantry and cavalry in two lines, facing outwards, thus affording a strong protection to everything contained in the enclosure. The power of the imagination can scarcely figure to itself the sudden transformation that takes place on these occasions, when an Indian camp exhibits, with the effect of an enchantment, the appearance of a lively and populous city amidst the wilds of solitude and on a dreary plain. In a short space the rough visage of war is changed to the reciprocal offices of confidence, and the fatigues of professional duty are forgotten amidst scenes of festivity. Throughout long and regular streets of shops, like the booths at an English fair, may be seen in, every direction all the bustling variety of trade, the relaxation of enjoyment, and the pursuits of pleasure. Here *sheroffs*, or moneychangers, are ready with their coin to accommodate those who are unprovided with the currency necessary for the purchase of the necessities or luxuries of life. In such a situation, where nothing more could well be expected than what serves to alleviate the present cravings of nature, every kind of luxury abounds; and while some shops allure the hungry passenger with boiled or parched rice, others exhibit a profusion of rich viands with spices, curry materials and confectionery, for the indulgence of a voluptuous appetite. European merchants, here called *sadawkers*, either by themselves or their native agents, are busily employed in vending wines, liquors, and groceries; while other traders exhibit for sale fine cloths, muslins, and rich cashmerian shawls. Here also are to be found goldsmiths and jewellers exercising their occupations and endeavouring to attract the fancy by a display of elegant ornaments, as though war had been deprived of its austerity, or that victory had already been decided. Besides these and various other traffickers, the camp exhibits the singular spectacle of female *quacks*, who practice cupping, sell drugs, and profess to cure disorders by charms. Nearly allied to these are the jugglers showing their dexterity by numerous arts of deception; and, to complete the motley assemblage, groups of dancing girls have their allotted station in the bazaar.

Captain Thorn enlarges at considerable length on the personal appearance, costume, accomplishments, and moral characteristics of these ladies, but the reader will perhaps have had enough of his description of the camp of the Grand Army. We shall see presently how the warriors who made themselves so comfortable on the march comported themselves in action, doubting not that a few months' campaigning enabled them to shake off some at least of their motley and cumbrous following.

On August 29 the army marched at four in the morning, and at once crossed into Maratha territory, leaving the baggage and bazaar at a village some four miles distant from Koil, information having been received that a hostile force was encamped between that town and the fort of Aligarh. The troops advanced to the attack at seven o'clock, and, on their presently coming into view, the enemy struck his camp and drew up his mounted troops in a strong position on a plain, the right resting on the fort of Aligarh, the left protected by some villages, and the front by a deep morass. The Maratha horse numbered about 9000, of whom from 4000 to 5000 were regulars; and some 2000 infantry were posted in villages in the vicinity of the fort. General Lake obviously had no choice but to attack the Maratha left, and this he did without hesitation, making the necessary flank movement with a confidence and steadiness which had an immediate effect. The guns of the fortress kept up a heavy fire on the British force during the flank march, but with little effect. On reaching the point where deployment was possible, the cavalry, led by the General in person, formed into two lines and advanced rapidly to the attack, supported by three or four lines of infantry. The Maratha horse were so intimidated by this regular and determined advance, and so hampered by the swampy ground in their front (which, although it protected them from a direct attack, also prevented them from making a counter-attack during the progress of Lake's flank movement), that they tamely fell back under the walls of the fortress. The British cavalry closely followed them up, the great crowd of horsemen of the two armies causing a dense cloud of dust to arise, which prevented the fire of the fort guns, even at this close range, from being effective. So demoralised were the Maratha horse by this rapid attack that Perron was unable to rally them, and they presently broke into a flight that quickly carried them beyond the reach of the British cavalry. Perron's bodyguard, a fine body of horsemen, alone maintained its formation, and escorted the General from the field in the direction of Agra.

General Lake now established his army hard by the town of Koil, encamping the troops on the north side of the town, which thus guarded the right flank of the camp: the left flank, being *en l'air*, was thrown back. Lake himself took up his residence in General Perron's fine house, the *Sahib Bagh*, which was midway between Koil and the fortress of Aligarh, and consequently about a mile from the front of his camp. When abandoning Aligarh and its garrison to their fate, which, indeed, he could not help doing, Perron urged his son-in-law, Colonel Pedron, the commandant of the fortress, to make a determined defence, promising to return presently at the head of the entire Maratha army and to drive away the English. Perron's letter was written in the somewhat theatrical style dear to Frenchmen, and so derided by the matter-of-fact Englishmen of two years ago. "Remember," wrote Perron, "that you are a Frenchman, and let no action of yours tarnish the character of your nation. I hope in a few days to send back the English general as fast, or faster than he came. Make yourself perfectly easy on this subject. Either the Emperor's army or that of General Lake shall find a grave before the fort of Allyghur. Do your duty and defend the fort while one stone remains upon another. Once more, remember your nation. The eyes of millions are fixed upon you."

Perron, however, on arriving at Agra found himself unable to fulfil his promise. He had for some time been on bad terms with his Maratha master; and Sindhia had, not long previously, actually insulted him in durbar. Several of the more prominent Maratha officers were desirous of taking Perron's place at the head of the army; and, more dangerous still, he had a treacherous rival in one of his own race, Louis Bourquin, the commander of the 1st Brigade of Sindhia's regular army.

Bourquin, whose record as a soldier was much inferior to that of Perron, made such effective use of his General's absence from Agra, and of his defeat outside Aligarh, that he now succeeded in procuring Perron's dismissal and his own promotion to a short-lived command.

General Lake, having disposed of Perron and his cavalry, had now to decide on his course of action with regard to Aligarh, and, having determined that he would not leave so strong a post in his rear, he decided to attack it promptly, and if possible to carry it by a *coup-de-main*. From his lack of siege material he could, in fact, take no other course. Knowing, however, that in all probability such action would result in a heavy loss of life, and particularly of Europeans, in whom his army was so dangerously weak, Lake endeavoured to persuade Colonel Pedron to surrender. He entered into a correspondence of five days' duration, and found Pedron much inclined to come to terms. The second-in-command of the fortress, a Rajput officer named Baji Rao, was, however, made of sterner stuff, and finally put an abrupt end to the peace negotiations by placing Colonel Pedron in arrest, assuming the command, and defying Lake to do his worst. Baji Rao was right, for he now had in his charge nearly all the reserve stores of the Maratha army, including some 300 guns of various calibres, great quantities of powder and shot, and large supplies of uniform of French pattern, and other necessaries. So essential an arsenal should not, he felt, be tamely surrendered. The fortress of Aligarh, too, was immensely strong. It had been selected by Perron as his headquarters on account of its natural advantages of position, and for years the most skilled French engineers had laboured to make it impregnable. The plain in the midst of which it stands, being intersected by swamps, becomes so inundated during the rainy season as to render the fort unapproachable by ordinary siege operations. As for a coup-de-main, the walls were of great height and strength, not to be quickly breached by the weak artillery of Lake's army; the ditch had a breadth varying from 100 to 200 feet and a depth of 32 feet; even in the dry season it had a minimum depth of 10 feet of water; the only entrance into the fort was so guarded by batteries as to be most difficult to force, and would indeed have been inaccessible had the commandant cut away a narrow bank which traversed the moat and carried a roadway into the fort. This precaution was not taken, doubtless from over-confidence and from a reliance on the promise of relief from Agra. Finally, the garrison was numerous and brave, consisting of 3000 infantry, 200 artillerymen, and a regiment of cavalry. 500 of the infantry were recruits, but fought as bravely as the rest.

The five days occupied in negotiation had not been unwelcome to the British force. On the evening of August 29 Lake had found his troops much exhausted: they had been under arms and in movement for many hours in great heat, and, even in the tents, after Perron's retreat, the thermometer had marked over 100 degrees. By September 3, however, they were much refreshed, and Lake having determined on an assault on the following morning, proceeded to select the storming-party and its commander.

His choice fell upon Colonel the Hon. William Monson, 76th Regiment, Brigadier of the 1st Brigade, a soldier of approved gallantry, who was naturally permitted to form the assaulting column from his own regiments. His column was thus composed: four companies 76th Regiment, under Major M'Leod, the officer commanding the regiment; the 1st Battalion 4th Native Infantry ; and four companies 17th Native Infantry. The remainder of the 1st Brigade was held in readiness to reinforce, and in the course of the attack the 2nd Battalion 4th Native Infantry was, in fact, brought up.

During the night of September 3 two batteries, each of four 18-pounders, were constructed by Captains Robertson and Greene, under the supervision of Lieut.-Colonel Horsford—one under cover of a village, and the other concealed by the trees of the Sahib Bagh, General Perron's house, now occupied by Lake. The fire of these batteries was intended to keep' down the fire from the walls of Aligarh during the assault. The stormers, headed by Colonel Monson, and guided by Mr Lucan, an English officer who had recently left the Maratha service in accordance with Lord Wellesley's proclamation, left camp at three o'clock in the morning of September 4, and, after a cautious advance, arrived unseen and unheard at a point within 400 yards of the only gateway of the fortress. Here they halted to wait for dawn. During the halt an officer crept forward to make a close reconnaissance, and found a Maratha picquet, sixty to seventy strong, smoking and talking round a fire in front of the gateway. A party of the 76th was now sent forward with the design of driving-this picquet through the gateway and entering with them. The men of the 76th attacked, however, with such impetuosity and suddenness that the whole picquet was slain, not a man escaping to tell the tale. The noise of the struggle or scuffle was heard by the sentries on the ramparts, who opened a brisk but unaimed fire for a time; but no notice being taken of their fire, it presently ceased, as they imagined that the sounds they had heard had been caused by the repulse of some rash patrol from the British lines. On the firing of the morning gun at Lake's camp the covering batteries, by arrangement, opened a heavy fire on the dimly seen walls of Aligarh, and Monson and his stormers advanced rapidly towards the gateway. When within 100 yards of the entrance they came upon a small and newly constructed work, mounting three 6-pounders. So rapid was the rush of stormers that the Maratha gunners were unable to fire a round in defence of the breast-work, but fled with the remainder of the garrison into the fort. The companies of the 76th hotly pursued them, again hoping to steal an entrance into the fortress; but those guarding the gate were by now on the alert, and the 76th found the gate closed, and immediately came under a destructive fire from several directions.

Two scaling-ladders were instantly brought up and placed

in position, and the grenadier company of the 76th, headed by Major M'Leod, the commanding officer of the regiment, endeavoured to mount the walls. They were, however, repulsed by pikemen, so this attempt also failed. The storming-party, nothing daunted, maintained their ground with grim determination, while as a last resort guns were brought up to blow in the gate. A 6-pounder was first used without effect, and afterwards, after some delay and great exertion, a 12-pounder was run up, which on the fifth or sixth discharge burst the gate open.

These operations occupied fully twenty minutes, during which time the stormers, crowded into a small space and exposed to a close fire, to which they could make no effective reply, lost heavily. Nor were their losses confined to those inflicted on them by the heavy guns, wall-pieces, and muskets from several parapets and walls which commanded their position, for numbers of the brave defenders of the fortress swarmed down the scaling-ladders and attacked them, sword or spear in hand, an incident rarely paralleled in war.[1]

In those fatal twenty minutes all the officers of the companies of the 76th were killed or wounded, and the casualties of the small column were so heavy that the 2nd Battalion 4th Native Infantry was brought up to reinforce it.

---

1. During the gallant defence of Vellore in 1781 against the army of Tippu of Mysore and his French allies, a prolonged attack was made on an outlying fort garrisoned by one hundred Madras Sepoys under two English subalterns. This small body of men held their own, during a persistent siege of five weeks' duration, "the enemy's artillery being well served, his infantry and investing force overwhelming; but the steady determined defence made by Lieutenants Champness and Parr, with a garrison entirely native, foiled and repulsed every assault. On one occasion the ladders were planted and ascended by the enemy, who were driven off with much slaughter, and the garrison following the gallant Lieutenant Parr, descended by them and became the assailants on the retreating foe, who, after a close and determined encounter with the bayonet, were dislodged from their position near the breach."

Among those of the storming-party severely wounded was its commander, Colonel Monson, the bone of whose arm was broken by the thrust of a pike.

The outer gate having at last been burst open, the stormers advanced at a run under a very heavy and close, but confused, fire to a second gate, which was easily broken down. A third gate, reached in like manner, was rushed, while the crowd of retreating Marathas prevented its being shut. The fourth and last gate, distant 500 yards from the outer one, was, however, closed, and though Captain Shipton of the artillery, who had been wounded during the advance, gallantly brought up his twelve-pounder, the gate defied his efforts.

Major M'Leod, however, a cool and determined soldier, forced the wicket, and the stormers made their way to the ramparts, where ensued all slaughter grim and great. The garrison of Aligarh maintained their brave defence for nearly an hour, and their loss in killed was stated to be no less than 2000 men, the surface of the ditch being thickly covered with the floating bodies of those who were shot or drowned while endeavouring to swim across it. Those who succeeded in crossing were, for the most part, cut down by the 27th Light Dragoons, for they refused to surrender. Quarter was given to those of the garrison who accepted it, and they were set at liberty by order of General Lake.

Colonel Pedron, the deposed governor, was brought a prisoner before Lake. He was found to be "an elderly man, clad in a green jacket with gold lace and epaulets."

Baji Rao, the brave Maratha chief, was among the slain.

The British casualties, so heavy during the check at the outer gate, were surprisingly light during the triumphant rush through the remaining defences. The killed numbered 55, of whom 6 were officers; and the wounded 205, of whom 11 were officers—a total of 260 casualties. The proportion of casualties to strength in the 76th Regiment was very high as compared with the native portion of the storming-party, yet the latter behaved extremely well.

Thus fell the fortress of Aligarh, believed by every native of India to be impregnable, as indeed it would have been had the care and vigilance of the defenders equalled their courage.

It may well be imagined with what anxiety Lake, who watched the assault from the battery in the Sahib Bagh, witnessed the check at the outer gateway. There stood by him, during those anxious twenty minutes, which seemed as long as so many hours, a cool and sympathetic observer in the person of James Skinner, perhaps the best soldier of mixed blood who ever served England.

Skinner tells us that when the stormers were checked and came under the terrible fire from the bastions and walls ("one of the heaviest fires of musketry and great guns I have seen," writes Skinner, who had seen many), General Lake feared that the assault had failed. When the gateway was forced, the 76th rushed through it with a great shout. As soon as he heard the shout the countenance of Lake changed from anxiety to joy, and he called out with the greatest delight, "The fort is ours!" and turning to Skinner (who had joined the British army from the Maratha service a few days before) asked him what he thought of European fighting. Skinner replied that "no forts in Hindustan could stand against it"—an answer which may have had unhappy results. "Then," adds Skinner, "spurring his horse, he galloped to the gate. But when he saw his heroes lying thick there, the tears came to his eyes. 'It is the fate of good soldiers,' he said."

Skinner concludes his narrative with the testimony, highly honourable coming from so experienced a soldier, that the courage displayed by the 76th surpassed all he had ever seen, and every idea he had formed of soldiering.

In the evening the bodies of the European slain were interred with great solemnity, those of the native soldiers being, of course, disposed of by their co-religionists as was meet for them. The five officers of the 76th were buried in front of the colour-guard of their regiment, General Lake and his staff, and all officers off duty, attending the procession, during which the band played the "Dead March," and minute guns were fired from the batteries. These seemly marks of respect for the brave and faithful dead can no longer be paid in war, and this record of old customs may therefore be of interest.

Lake reported his success to the Governor-General in a formal despatch, and entered into further particulars in the following hasty but interesting letter written on the day of the assault:

Camp at Coel
September 4, 1803.
My Lord,—By my official letter which accompanies this, you will, I am sorry to say, perceive that I have lost a great many valuable officers, and that unfortunately Colonel Monson, who behaved most gloriously, has received a most severe wound in the arm from, a pike. The bone, I understand, is broken high up; but Mr Lenny and the other surgeons who have examined it have hopes that he may recover without amputation. I cannot say too much of the conduct of Colonel Monson upon this occasion; he is a most serious loss to the army. Your lordship may easily conceive what I feel at his misfortune and the loss of so many brave men.

As I told your lordship in my letter of the 1st instant, I had tried every method to prevail upon these people to give up the fort, and offered a very large sum of money; but they were determined to hold out, which they did most obstinately, and I may say most gallantly. In short, my lord, from the extraordinary strength of the place, and being obliged to win it inch by inch, it being so determinedly defended, in my opinion British valour never shone more conspicuous. I think this action will strike terror into the natives, and prevent us some trouble. I trust your lordship will agree with me in thinking that I have done right in gaining this fort at any rate, as, in the first place, it was so strong that I could not look upon my army safe with such a fort in my rear; in the second place, it would have given the natives a very poor opinion of our troops; and in the third place, I am convinced that after a regular siege we must have had the same difficulties to encounter. The strength of the place cannot be described but by a drawing, which shall be sent down to you as soon as it can be prepared; a seventy-four might sail in the ditch. The engineer and Colonel Horsford both think that after a breach had been made we should have lost as many men as we now have, besides what would have fallen during a siege, which would have lasted nearly a month.

All these points being considered, the delay that would have been caused in the execution of your orders, and the certainty of giving spirit to the Maratha chiefs, who would then have been inclined to flock to the Frenchman's standard, I feel happy at having gained the fort, which stood out for more than an hour. A more anxious time I never experienced; the fire was tremendous, and nothing, from the strong way in which the natives were posted with all their advantages, but British soldiers would have effected the business. I have wrote more than I intended, and I must beg you will pardon me for being so prolix, but really my mind is so much agitated from the loss of so many excellent men that I hardly know what I do.

It appears, I am sorry to say, that poor Monson's wound may be attended with danger, as in the event of amputation, danger is always to be apprehended in this country; but I trust and hope I shall be able to send you a better account of him to-morrow.

P.S.—I have only to add that, without the fort of Alyghur, we could not have had the entire possession of the Doab; indeed, till it was ours, we were liable to be driven out of it at any time.

The news of the capture of Aligarh was received with great pleasure by Lord Wellesley, who eulogised in his General Order of September 15, 1803, the "alacrity and valour" with which Lake decided on the assault. The Governor-General also praised in befitting terms those officers whom Lake had mentioned as having distinguished themselves, beginning, of course, with Colonel Monson. It may be here recorded that Lake by no means followed the routine of the period in his "mentions in despatches," for instead of merely recommending for reward the staff and commanding officers, then the almost invariable custom, he, on this and other occasions, was guided strictly by merit. Three captains of artillery received special mention—two for service with the covering batteries, and Captain Shipton, who blew in the gates; but the most marked praise of all was awarded to Lucan, the gallant Irishman who, at the imminent risk of his life, led the assaulting column. Terrible indeed would have been Lucan's fate if captured, as it was unfortunately his destiny to prove later in the campaign.

The risks taken by Lucan were fully recognised and promptly rewarded by Lord Wellesley, who conferred on him a money reward of Rs. 24,000 and a lieutenant's commission in the 74th Regiment.

A little space must now be given to the movements of General Perron's troops after their hurried retreat from outside Aligarh. Of the 9000 or more mounted men present on that occasion, nearly half either dispersed or broke away in small parties and returned to their own districts. On reaching Hatras, Perron intrusted the command of 5000 good men, who still maintained their discipline, to Captain Fleury, one of his best French officers, and ordered him to harry the country towards Cawnpore and to hamper General Lake's movements. Perron himself, with his bodyguard, continued his retirement to Agra, to which place he had sent his family and private property : what befell him there will presently be related.

Captain Fleury at first carried out his orders with some success, for moving against Shikohabad, a small outpost on the Company's frontier in the Etawah district, he attacked it on September 2. Shikohabad was held by a weak garrison of five companies of the 11th Native Infantry, with one gun, under Lieut.-Colonel Coningham, and the position has no natural strength.

Fleury made repeated attacks from four in the morning till two in the afternoon, but without success. He then withdrew and called up reinforcements, with which he again attacked two days later. Colonel Coningham's force had held out stoutly, but he and nearly all his officers had been wounded, his small force had sustained over sixty casualties, ammunition was running short, and no relief appeared probable. In these circumstances Coningham thought a capitulation justified. The small British force was permitted by Fleury to retire from Shikohabad with its gun and other arms on engaging to take no further part in the war against Sindhia. Captain Thorn adds to the above facts a statement that the wife of an English officer was carried off. There appears to be no record of her fate.

On hearing of the attack on Shikohabad, General Lake at once despatched the 3rd Cavalry Brigade, under Colonel Macan, to deal with Fleury's force. Macan, a bold and enterprising Irishman, marched rapidly in search of the Maratha horse; but Fleury, who had sustained heavy losses in the two days' fighting at Shikohabad, showed no desire for further fighting in spite of his greatly superior strength.

Falling back on Agra, Fleury's force eventually made a precipitate retreat across the Jumna, accompanied in their flight by the garrison of Ferozabad, a fortified village only twenty-four miles distant from Agra. Macan, following in hot pursuit, took possession of Ferozabad, capturing there nine guns, a large quantity of grain, and some cattle.

Macan's brigade, with complete confidence, carried on its independent operations round Agra for twelve days, until on September 17 it was joined by the 8th Light Dragoons and three battalions of the 2nd Infantry Brigade under Colonel Clarke. The command of the combined force was then assumed by Colonel Thomas Pakenham Vandeleur, the senior Lieutenant-Colonel of the 8th Light Dragoons. The 8th were now making their first appearance in the campaign, having only recently arrived in India. They had been mounted during the month of July on horses provided by the Nawab-Wazir of Oudh.

Colonel Vandeleur, finding that no further enterprise was to be feared from Fleury, now proceeded along the eastern bank of the Jumna to a point opposite Muttra, in order to cross the river there and rejoin the main army, whose movements must now be described.

A halt of two days at Aligarh, after its capture, sufficed General Lake to restore the broken defences and establish a garrison of one battalion of Native Infantry.

On September 7 he marched away to Sumna, in the direction of Delhi. Here Lake received a letter from General

Perron, stating that he had quitted the service of Sindhia, and asking permission to take refuge under British protection at Lucknow. This important step, for which General Perron has been unjustly stigmatised as a traitor by some writers, was thus brought about. Perron, like his great predecessor De Boigne, was well known by the Maratha leaders to be opposed to war with the British; and this knowledge, as soon as war became inevitable, rendered his position impossible. He was no longer trusted by Sindhia, and the fact was well known to the officers, and indeed to the whole army, which he had formerly held completely under his control. Perron's removal from his command was obviously imminent, and on the outbreak of war, the only question was at what moment and in what manner the removal would come about. Among those who most loudly and constantly asked this question was the man who desired to supplant him, Louis Bourquin, a fellow-countryman and dependant of Perron's, but a man of much lower type, who was now brigadier of the 1st Brigade of the Maratha army. No sooner had the news of Perron's defeat before Aligarh reached Delhi than Bourquin declared Perron a traitor, and induced, first, his own brigade, and subsequently the whole army at Delhi, to proclaim him as their commander. This disloyal conduct was opposed by Geslin, also a Frenchman, the commander of the 2nd Brigade; and by Drugeon, also French, the commandant of the citadel of Delhi.

A full narrative of the intrigues resulting in Perron's deposition may be read in Compton's *European Military Adventurers of Hindustan*, but it must here be sufficient to say that treachery was triumphant, that the loyal European officers who stood by General Perron were placed in confinement, and that by September 9 Bourquin found himself in command of an imposing force of 18 battalions of infantry, a large body of cavalry, including Fleury's late corps of

Hindustani Mohammedans, and 110 guns. Fleury himself was now on his way with General Perron to Lucknow, accompanied by five other officers who had declined further service after the deposition of Perron, but had not taken an active part in the dispute for command.

With this strong body of experienced and brave soldiers Bourquin might be expected to prove a formidable foe; but it must be recognised that the confidence of the Maratha troops was inevitably shaken by the patent intrigues and dissensions among their foreign officers, and also that in the day of battle they would assuredly go into action under Bourquin without the feeling of confidence with which the proved skill of Perron would have inspired them.

Lake's army, on the other hand, excited and encouraged by the rapid triumphs of Aligarh, and believing implicitly in the capacity of their commander to surmount all difficulties and to defy all odds, moved forward to meet their enemy with a light heart.

On September 8 Lake again advanced to the town of Kurja, the distance covered in this and the preceding march being thirty miles. So great was the alarm produced among the Marathas by the fall of Aligarh, that the fort of Kurja, which contained a great store of grain, was abandoned before the arrival of the British army. On September 9 Sikandra reached, and on the following day the army made a short march to the westward.

On September 11, destined to be the last day of many brave soldiers' lives, the force marched as usual at 3 a.m., and by 11 o'clock had covered eighteen miles and had crossed the river Hindan. Lake heard in the course of the march that Bourquin had left Delhi and crossed the Jumna during the night, and it was certain that he could not be far off, although the cavalry had failed to observe his line of approach. The march had been an easy one, for the morning temperature was now moderate; but the troops were fatigued from the great accuracy of movement rendered necessary by the square formation, already described, in which the army moved. Lake apparently believed that Bourquin was holding back, and, seeing that his own troops were weary and had made a sufficiently long march, he now j ordered them to pitch camp and cook their dinners. The ground selected was an open space about a mile beyond the Hindan, and only some six miles distant from Delhi, though the broad Jumna still intervened.

Bourquin, whatever his defects as a soldier, at least showed no unreadiness to fight. He was aware that Lake's army was weakened both by his casualties at Aligarh and the garrison that he had left there, and also by his having detached half his weak force of cavalry in pursuit of Fleury's raiders, and he now came confidently forward to attack the British army wherever he might find them.

As has been explained, he did find them comfortably settling down into camp, and therefore at a considerable disadvantage.

The early stages of the action, called by historians the battle of Delhi, have not been very clearly described, but apparently neither army was at first aware of its enemy's position. Lake certainly did not know that Bourquin was coming straight towards him, nor would Bourquin have lost the opportunity which the disadvantageous circumstances of the British force offered him had he known exactly where they were and what they were doing.

Just after Lake's camp had been pitched, a few Maratha mounted skirmishers opened fire on the British outposts. No great notice of their attack was at first taken, but, the enemy being rapidly reinforced, the British "grand-guard" or reserve of the outposts turned out. General Lake immediately afterwards rode to the front with three regiments of cavalry—all the mounted troops that he had with his army that day—in order to make a personal reconnaissance.

Driving back the Maratha horse who had given him timely warning of Bourquin's proximity, Lake followed them up for two miles, when he found Bourquin's army drawn up on rising ground, the infantry in line and strongly entrenched, and their front further protected by their numerous artillery. Either flank of the position was guarded by one of the large *jhils*, or marshes, so common in India during the rainy season, and the cavalry was posted in rear of each *jhil* in positions favourable for checking any turning movement that Lake might attempt to make.

Lake quickly grasped the situation, and realised that a frontal attack was forced upon him. In view, however, of his own weakness and of the great strength of the Maratha position, he decided to attempt to draw Bourquin from his entrenchments. Sending orders to his camp for the infantry and artillery to get under arms and, leaving the tents standing, to advance with all speed, Lake proceeded with great coolness to occupy the attention of the Maratha army.

With this design he for a time held his ground with the cavalry brigade, disregarding the heavy loss in men and horses inflicted on them by the Maratha artillery. The British infantry and artillery having to get under arms and into battle formation (an operation that, at that period, was in no circumstances hurriedly or negligently performed), and having subsequently to march two miles to the point where Lake was manoeuvring with the cavalry brigade, was unable to arrive on the scene of action in less than an hour from the receipt of the order. During this interval Lake, while deliberately exposing his mounted troops, took, as was his wont, a full share of their risks. His horse was shot under him, upon which his son, Major George Lake, dismounted and gave him his own charger, himself mounting the horse of a trooper who had been killed. The General's second charger having been brought up, he mounted it, but it presently was also killed under him.

By this time the British infantry and artillery were advancing, but unseen as yet by the Marathas, who were greatly excited by the success of their artillery fire in causing loss to Lake's cavalry. Lake, seeing the approach of his main body, now ordered his cavalry to feign a retreat—a hazardous movement, which this weak mounted force carried out with fine steadiness and regularity until, on approaching their infantry, they suddenly swept outwards at a gallop to both flanks, thus clearing the front of the infantry, and then formed up forty yards in rear of the right wing. This rapid movement, taking the place of the former slow retirement, was believed by the Marathas to betoken a flight, and they instantly hurried forward from their entrenchments, taking with them all their artillery, "shouting and exulting," writes Thorn, an eye-witness, "as if the victory had been already secured." A body of Sikh cavalry also advanced and threatened the British right.

Lake's infantry, consisting of only eight battalions, some of which were considerably under strength, were formed in one line, the cavalry furnishing their only support; and Lake, placing himself in front of the right battalion, the 76th, ordered an advance straight on the enemy. The picquets, commanded by Lieut.-Colonel White of the 16th Native Infantry, an officer who repeatedly distinguished himself during the campaign, moved as skirmishers before the line, and showed both skill and courage during the attack.

Major-Generals Ware and St John led their respective wings, and with General Lake headed the advance, which was performed with perfect coolness and steadiness, no answer being made by the infantry to the very heavy fire of round, grape, and chain shot by which they were assailed.

Colonel Horsford placed four guns under cover of a village near the left of the British line, and opened as heavy a fire as possible to aid the infantry advance; while a portion of the cavalry, with two galloper guns, advanced to the right front to hold off the body of Sikh cavalry which was threatening that flank. This body is said to have been 5000 strong, but the Sikh cavalry of this date was of poor quality.

The British line moved on in perfect formation and in strict silence until it came within 100 yards of the Maratha guns, many of which were of large calibre, and all of an efficiency most unusual in the native armies of India. At this close range every gun opened a heavy fire of grape, when the British line was ordered to fire a volley and charge with the bayonet. Headed by the three generals and all the staff and regimental officers, the line, having fired, rushed forward with such impetuosity that the Marathas instantly broke and fled in all directions. It is stated that Bourquin was one of the first to quit the field.

Lake at once ordered the infantry to halt and break into company columns, the cavalry with their galloper guns promptly charging through the intervals thus formed and taking up the pursuit. The greater part of the hapless Marathas fled before the cavalry in defenceless flight towards the place where they had crossed the Jumna on the previous night, and were eventually driven into the river, in whose waters great numbers of them were drowned or slain by the fire of the galloper guns.

Lake, observing that a portion of the flying enemy, with some of the lighter guns, were making for the river to his left front, at once wheeled his infantry in that direction and pursued the Marathas into the ravines and Broken ground, in which they attempted to find concealment. Here also the resistance was brief, and the demoralised enemy were quickly put to flight, leaving their guns and stores to the victors.

The battle of Delhi, as the action has been named by historians, was a fine achievement, reflecting the highest honour both on the British troops and their commander. Lake's small force, hardly greater in strength than a single brigade, marched and fought, with a very brief rest, for no less than sixteen hours, from three in the morning until seven in the evening, and during at least six hours in great heat, The conduct of all branches throughout this long trial of endurance and determination was equal to that exhibited in any exploit of British arms.

If, however, the troops, British and native alike, deserve this high praise, and a consideration of the circumstances will surely lead to that conclusion, it is also clear that the commander showed very high qualities. Lake was undoubtedly taken by surprise at the outset of the action, for which circumstance he cannot be absolved from blame; but his bold and confident handling of his troops during the rapid progress of the battle bears comparison with that of his great subordinate, Arthur Wellesley. Lake's tactics, judged by the cold eye of the pedant, were doubtless open to criticism, yet they were justified by the circumstances of the case; they enabled him to cope with a most difficult situation, and they were rewarded by a sticking success. The great discrepancy in numbers (he had but 4500 men in action against the 19,000 of Bourquin) would have given pause to many a bold spirit. Lake, however, always acted on the principle that safety and victory rested with the attack; he was aware of the disintegrating effect on the Maratha army of the loss of all the European officers in whom they had so long trusted, and he had a just confidence in the moral of his own troops. The result justified his action.

Fighting against such odds, and under such conditions as have been described, the casualties of the British force were inevitably heavy. They were 461 in killed or wounded, or 10 per cent of the force engaged. Those of the 76th, the only European infantry regiment present, amounted to 137, of whom 33 were killed outright—a heavy addition to the losses which they had sustained at Aligarh. In the whole force, 16 British officers and 172 Europeans of other ranks were killed or wounded, or 40 per cent of the total casualties. This, as at Aligarh, was an unduly heavy proportion, showing both that Lake still carried out his principle of giving his European troops the toughest work, and that the Marathas concentrated their fire against them. The native regiments which suffered most heavily were the 2nd Battalion 4th Native Infantry with 91 casualties, and the 2nd Battalion 12th Native Infantry with 55. It may here be noted that the latter battalion, in spite of its numerical position, was actually the senior native battalion in the Bengal army, and had served at the battle of Plassy.

The losses of the Maratha army were never accurately ascertained, but the lowest estimate was 3000 men killed and wounded. Sixty-eight pieces of ordnance were captured on the field, all of good quality and fitted with elevating screws of the latest French pattern.

After the battle General Lake moved his army nearer to the Jumna and pitched camp opposite the city of Delhi, within view of whose lofty battlements the action had taken place. While arranging to cross the river and enter the Moghul capital, Lake addressed the following very brief despatch to Lord Wellesley:

Headquarters' Camp
near Delhi Ghaut
September 13, 1803
My Lord,—For your lordship's information I have the honour to enclose a list of the killed and wounded— officers and men of the army under my command—in the action of the 11th instant.

Your lordship will perceive that our loss has been very great; but when I consider that we moved on against an immense artillery, of nearly 100 pieces of cannon, and many of a very large calibre, under as heavy a fire as I have ever been witness to; and that this fire was directed against a line, consisting, on the must correct calculation, of not more than 4500 men, including cavalry, artillery, and infantry; and that we were opposed by upwards of four times that number, it is no longer a matter of surprise. It is necessary to remark that we had only one brigade of cavalry, consisting of the 27th Light Dragoons and the 2nd and 3rd Regiments of Native Cavalry; the other brigades being detached for the protection of our own provinces.

The more I reflect on the glorious affair of the 11th, the more forcibly I feel the bravery and intrepidity displayed by every individual composing my army. I cannot find words to express my feelings on this occasion, nor can I sufficiently lament the loss of many brave fellows who have fallen.

I have the honour to be, my lord, your lordship's most faithful humble servant,

G. Lake

On December 14 the army crossed the Jumna and encamped outside Delhi, General Bourquin and four of his French officers surrendering the same day.

The power of the French state, as Lord Wellesley had justifiably called the Doab, was now broken, its army broken and dispersed, and its chief officers in British custody. The emperor, Shah Alam, gladly accepted British protection, and agreed to the appointment of a Resident at his Court. These results came of seventeen days of marching and fighting, and seldom has a force, numerically so weak, done better work in so short a period.

Lord Wellesley, who well understood the appreciation felt by native soldiers of visible marks of distinction, ordered the presentation of honorary standards or colours to the corps who had most distinguished themselves at the capture of Aligarh and the battle of Delhi. Rightly feeling that this high honour would be enhanced in value if shared by the European corps, Lord Wellesley conferred the same distinction on the 27th Light Dragoons and the 76th Regiment. The brave 27th have long disappeared from the Army List, but the 76th, now the 2nd Battalion of the Duke of Wellington's Regiment, still carry the additional colours, emblazoned with the words "Lake and Victory," and still claim the honourable if unofficial title of the "Hindustan Regiment."

On receiving General Lake's description of his victory, Lord Wellesley hastened to write his thanks in the following glowing terms, which, we may be sure, went home to the warm heart of his Commander-in-Chief:

Soonamooker
Off Barrackpoor
September 30, 1803.
My dear Sir,—I avail myself of the first moment of my recovery from sickness to offer you my most cordial congratulations on the glorious victory of the 11th, and on its decisive and propitious consequences. An event more honourable to the British arms never occurred in any part of the world, and in India the conduct and result of the action stand without parallel. Much as I feel indebted to the merits of your army, justice, universal consent of all parties, and the plain evidence of indisputable fact concur to point my principal attention to your matchless energy, ability, and valour. You have formed the army to this illustrious and extraordinary achievement, and to your

personal exertion must be attributed the promptitude, skill, and irresistible intrepidity which marked our operations on that memorable day. The result must be the utter extinction of the last vestige of French influence in India, the defeat of the ambitious and rapacious views of the Maratha confederates, and a speedy peace with ample indemnity and security to the allies. You are entitled to the highest honours and rewards which your country and your king can bestow; from me, as the representative of both in India, you will receive every testimony which I can afford in my public capacity of my admiration of your conduct, and of the high value and consideration which I attach to your eminent services. My private gratitude cannot be expressed, nor is it possible to form a hope of discharging such a debt according to my estimation of its extent. My life, however protracted, could not furnish the means of satisfying my sentiments on this occasion; but whatever can be expected from the most cordial, firm, and zealous respect, affection and attachment, must ever be commanded by you from me, and from every person connected with me.

Ever, my dear sir, yours most faithfully and affectionately, with the most cordial esteem and attachment,
Wellesley

Before this generous and appreciative letter had reached General Lake, the "matchless energy" of which the Governor-General speaks had secured yet another triumph to our arms. The great fortress of Agra, "the key of Hindustan," had fallen.

Before describing the operations which led to that result, we must pause in our narrative to describe briefly the strange scenes which Lake and his officers witnessed at

Delhi. Two days after the arrival of the British army before the walls of the capital, the victorious General was received with all practicable ceremony at the faded Court of the emperor. Shah Alam, who professed great joy at the removal of his Maratha and French masters, announced his wish to confer the highest available distinction on his deliverer, and with this design in view it was arranged that Lake should be led into the imperial presence by no less a personage than Mirza Akbar Shah, the heir-apparent.

The Prince's arrival at Lake's camp was timed for noon on September 16, but with the unpunctuality that is considered essential to royal dignity in the East, Mirza Akbar Shah was three hours late. It was consequently near sunset when the joint cavalcade of the Commander-in-Chief and the imperial Prince arrived at the noble palace of Shah Jahan, the glory of Moghul architecture. They had found the streets of Delhi densely crowded with the population of that great though decayed city, and even the courts of the palace, themselves of great extent, were filled with spectators anxious to realise for themselves the coming restoration to something of its former splendour of the house of Taimur; for to the people of Delhi the Moghul dynasty was very dear, as is its memory to the present day.

The progress of Lake and his cavalcade through the crowded assemblage had therefore been slow, and on that account had appeared to them stately, and not until the moment of their introduction to the royal hall of audience did the Englishmen realise how great had been the change from the past magnificence of Delhi. No squalor could deprive the exquisite Diwan-i-Khas of its beauty of outline and colour, and Lake and his following well knew that in these very courts which they traversed the eyes of ambassadors from the monarchs of the West had been dazzled by the pomp of Indian majesty, that there great tributary princes had bowed like the lowest slaves, and the simplest expression of the monarch's will had passed as a law to an empire vast as modern Europe.

"But now," writes Thorn, rising to unwonted eloquence, "such is the vanity of earthly grandeur and the uncertainty of mortal power, the descendant of the great Akbar, and the victorious Aurangzeb, was found, an object of pity, blind and aged, stripped of authority, and reduced to poverty, seated under a small tattered canopy, the fragment of royal state and the mockery of human pride."

Lake was received by the emperor with the utmost cordiality, and by the courtiers with; every demonstration of gratitude. It was true that the arrival of his army and the assumption of a British protectorate over the wreck of the Moghul empire promised in reality no more, to the emperor and his subjects than a change of masters. That reflection would come later; now the defeat and flight of the hated Marathas was the first thought in every mind, and joy and gratitude prevailed.

The emperor had nothing to bestow on his deliverer but titles of honour, and these fell upon Lake in a lavish flood. The highest title of the empire had already been conferred on Sindhia, but the second in precedence was available, and thenceforth Lake had every right to style himself "Sword of the State, Hero of the land, Lord of the age, Victorious in war." Even in plain English there is dignity in these titles; judge then of their effect when recited in sonorous Persian.

To the practical and unimaginative minds of a later age these high-sounding titles, emanating from the ruined sovereign of a bankrupt empire, may sound farcical and empty, but they bore another meaning to General Lake. To him, courtier as well as soldier, and emphatically a royalist, the emperor was a legitimate sovereign of a lineage second to none in the world. Shah Alam, rich or poor, was "the Great Moghul," the descendant and representative of Aurangzeb, Shah Jahan, Akbar, and Babar, and therefore a monarch from whom titles might be received by any subject with gratitude and pride. Not only did Lake value his Moghul titles, and frankly acknowledge the fact in a letter to Lord Wellesley, but they (were the only reward that he would accept from Shah Alam, when the latter presently found the imperial treasury in a condition to which it had been a stranger during his lifetime at least, and offered a large sum of money to his deliverer.

Of Lake's disinterested and generous character we shall speak hereafter, but this is a fitting occasion to quote his statement that he had "ever held money in most sovereign contempt"—a sentiment that by no means all great commanders have shared with him.

Lake made no longer halt at Delhi than was required to rest his troops and to collect supplies for a fresh advance. Owing to the smallness of his force, he was unable to leave an adequate garrison behind him, but Colonel David Ochterlony, the officer selected by Lake for the post of Resident, was a host in himself, and Lieut.-Colonel Burn, the officer chosen to command the garrison of one battalion and four companies of Native Infantry, was also brave and capable. To strengthen Burn's inadequate force Colonel Ochterlony received orders to raise two battalions of *najibs* (men from distant states) from the disbanded sepoys of Bourquin's regiments. These were commanded by Lieutenants Birch and Woodville, two of the English officers formerly in the Maratha service. Eight squadrons of Fleury's Hindustani Horse entered the British service at the same time, and at their own request were placed under the command of James Skinner, an officer of mixed blood who, having been discharged from the Maratha service against his will by General Perron, had, as already mentioned, joined Lake before Aligarh.

Skinner, a daring and experienced soldier, who had seen much hard fighting in the wars between the Marathas and the Rajputs, was greatly trusted and respected by native soldiers, who had converted his name into Sikandar, by which designation he was well known throughout Hindustan. When the surrendered cavalry were drawn up for General Lake's inspection they observed Skinner riding among Lake's staff. Lake asked the troopers whom they would like as a commanding officer, expecting them to nominate a countryman of their own, but the sowars with one voice replied, "Give us Sikandar Sahib."

Skinner stipulated that neither he nor his men should be required to serve against Sindhia, and they were consequently not employed during the campaign of 1803. Their services in the following year will presently be recorded.

In leaving Ochterlony at Delhi, Lake was well aware that he was depriving himself of the best subordinate officer in his army—of the man, as he said, in whom he felt more confidence than in any officer he had met in India. David Ochterlony, who has so favourably impressed Lake, was now forty-five years of age. Born in North America of Scottish parents, he had entered the Bengal army in 1777, and established his reputation as a brave and capable soldier in the campaigns of Sir Eyre Coote against Haider Ali of Mysore and his French allies under Bussy. Ochterlony accompanied the Bengal detachment which, in 1781, marched, 1100 miles under Colonel Thomas Deane Pearse to join the Madras army and rendered valiant, services. Ochterlony, during this campaigns commanded the 24th Bengal Native Infantry at Cuddalore in 1783, and was at their head on the famous occasion when they crossed bayonets with a French infantry regiment and repulsed its attack. Ochterlony was wounded and taken prisoner in the charge. He had been promoted lieutenant-colonel in March 1803. We shall see presently how he justified the confidence reposed in him by Lake.

The Commander-in-Chief's new objective was the great fortress of Agra, known to the native world of India as "the key of Hindustan," and the army marched from Delhi on September 24 in high spirits and good health. The route taken lay along the left bank of the Jumna, and the heaviest of the guns it captured at the battle of Delhi were conveyed in boats down the river for the expected siege operations.

Four days after leaving Delhi, Lake, who had evidently been anxious to receive an assurance of Lord Wellesley's approval of his operations at Aligarh, was made happy by receipt of a private letter from the Governor-General. This, unfortunately, has not been preserved, but its purport may be gathered from the following reply, interesting as a revelation of Lake's warmth of heart and appreciation of kindness:

Urwali
September 29, 1803.
My Lord,—Your letter of the 15th instant reached me last night, couched in such terms of friendship and flattering approbation of my conduct as to leave me quite destitute of words to express my feelings and sensations upon the occasion, and I can only assure your lordship that, although I may be deficient in language to thank you for your abundant kindness towards me, my heart overflows with gratitude, and will, as long as I draw breath, ever glow with the warmest sentiments of attachment and affection for the confidence and powers you have so liberally and fully entrusted and reposed in me, and of which, I trust, you will never have cause to repent.

I accord with your lordship in thinking that the honour and interest of our country must certainly console us for the loss of so many brave men, when we consider the advantage of their achievements.

It affords me very peculiar satisfaction to perceive your lordship approves so entirely of my conduct in the capture of Alighar, as I stood alone in my opinion respecting the attack. I am now more than ever convinced it was perfectly right, as a long siege would have lost the country, and cost us, I do most firmly believe, a considerable number more lives.

I used every endeavour to avoid the effusion of human blood, which is a source of great satisfaction to my mind, as I think no man in my situation should wantonly throw away the lives of his own men, or inhumanly butcher those of his enemy. These sentiments will, I trust, plead my excuse to my God and my country, and entitle me to a continuance of your friendship and affection.

I have the honour to be, my dear lord, your most attached and devoted servant,

G. Lake

On October 2 the army arrived before the ancient and sacred city of Muttra, where it was joined by the detached force under Colonel Vandeleur, whose movements have already been described. On arrival at Muttra all the Hindu soldiers in the army were granted leave for the remainder of the day to enable them to worship at the holy city of Bindrabund, which is close to Muttra.

On October 3 the army marched half-way from Muttra to Agra, and at about two in the afternoon of October 4 it arrived before that city, passing near Sikandra, the beautiful tomb of the Emperor Akbar, and encamping on or about the site of the present cantonments. The city of

Agra was found to be surrounded by a wall, part of which still exists, and was commanded by the great fort built by Akbar in the reign of our Queen Elizabeth. The fort, which stands on the bank of the Jumna, has lofty walls and flanking towers of red sandstone, with a deep ditch provided with a *fausse-braie*.[1] It lies to the south-west of the city, and the walls of the latter abutted on the fort on two sides. To the south and south-west of the fort are a number of ravines running to the Jumna. About 250 yards from the fort, and inside the city, stands the Jamma Masjid, or Great Mosque, on an elevated site. General Lake's task in attacking Agra was somewhat complicated by the following circumstance.

In addition to the garrison of the fortress, consisting of 4000 men under Colonel George Hessing, a Dutch officer, there was, encamped on the glacis of the fort, a force some 7000 strong which had first to be dealt with. This body was composed of Perron's 5th Brigade, and of three battalions from the 2nd and 3rd Brigades. All three Brigades had been ordered up from the Deccan on war becoming imminent, but, owing to Lake's unexpectedly early commencement of operations, had arrived near Delhi just too late for the battle of September 11.

The seven battalions had marched to Agra and requested admission to the fortress, but had been excluded by the garrison, which had broken into rebellion. Hessing, the commandant, and Sutherland, the next senior officer, had been confined by the troops, and when Lake, wishing to save loss of life, summoned the garrison to surrender, he could obtain no answer from them. In these circumstances no serious resistance was to be expected from the garrison; but the seven battalions outside, which had with

---

1. "Fausse-braie"—works designed to bring fire on the assailants of the curtain of a fortress, at places not protected by fire prom the bastions.

them twenty-six pieces of ordnance, had maintained their discipline, and promised to offer a stout resistance.

They had taken up a strong position under the walls of the fortress, and held the town of Agra and a number of ravines which led from the river Jumna up to the glacis, which they also occupied. They were fighting, literally, with their backs to the wall, and Lake, who had no men to spare, saw that he would have no easy task in attacking them.

There were 4000 Maratha troops in the fortress, and should Lake attack the force on the glacis and town only, ignoring the garrison, there was a strong probability that the latter would seize the opportunity and take the British force at a disadvantage. Yet he could make no delay, for he was aware that at no great distance there was a force of seventeen battalions, also marching towards Agra from the Deccan, who might presently fall upon him.

Lake therefore took the only proper resolution—to attack simultaneously the town and the force outside the fortress, while holding the latter in check by a threatened assault. For the external attack he selected, as far as possible, regiments which had not been engaged at Aligarh and Delhi, or which had suffered the least severe losses in those actions, while with the remainder of his army he took up a fresh position which prohibited any sortie from the fortress.

On the morning of October 10 Brigadier-General Clarke was ordered to attack the town of Agra with the 2nd Brigade, while three battalions, the 1st Battalion 14th Native Infantry and 1st and 2nd Battalions 15th Native Infantry, under Lieut.-Colonel M'Culloch, were detailed to drive out the Maratha troops holding the ravines previously described.

M'Culloch's force attacked first with great spirit, and quickly overcoming the resistance of the Marathas, drove them from the ravines without much difficulty. Excited by their success, and, it is said, led on by the too impetuous courage of their officers, M'Culloch's battalions unfortunately exceeded their orders and pressed on to the glacis in hope of capturing the guns placed in battery there. In this attempt they came under a heavy fire of grape and musketry from the fort, and sustained severe losses.

The 2nd Brigade also found their task no easy one, two battalions becoming so discouraged at one period of the attack as to retreat to their starting-place. Happily the remaining unit of the brigade, a wing of the 16th Native Infantry, gallantly held its ground under Lieut.-Colonel White and Brigadier-General Clarke, who highly distinguished himself, was subsequently able to bring back to the attack the battalions which had retired, and finally to maintain possession of the town. In a letter written to Lord Wellesley while these operations were in progress, Lake said that the troops of the enemy had fought most desperately, and that they were supposed to be the best that Perron had. He added, however, that he intended to open his batteries against the fort, and that, as the ground was very favourable, he had no doubt of being able quickly to breach the walls. The ravines captured that day would serve as admirable approaches to the fortress.

Lake added an expression of opinion which has often been quoted, and which has value today although a great part of the native Indian army is now composed of races which rank among the highest of the fighting peoples of the world. "The sepoys," he wrote, "have behaved excessively well, but from my observation this day, as well as on every other, it is impossible to do great things in a gallant and quick style without Europeans; therefore if they do not in England think it necessary to send British troops in the proportion of one to three sepoy regiments, which is, in fact, as one to six" (the native regiments having each two battalions), " they will stand a good chance of losing their possessions if a French force once get a footing in India. You may perceive by the loss of European officers in sepoy regiments how necessary it is for them to expose them-selves—in short, everything has been done by the example and exertions of the officers."

Lake's anticipations as to the success of the day's opera-tions were fulfilled. By night the Maratha troops had all been driven from the town, and the twenty-six guns there and on the glacis had all been captured. The loss of the Marathas was 600 men, while that of Brigadiers-General Clarke and Lieut.-Colonel M'Culloch's battalions was 228 killed and wounded, including 2 officers killed and 7 wounded.

Three days later 2500 men, about half of the remain-ing Maratha force outside the fortress, surrendered and marched into the British camp, the other half swelling the garrison of the fort; and very early on the same morning (October 13) Lake attacked the fortress itself. Approaches had been constructed, as designed by Lake, by way of the ravines captured on the 10th, and a breaching battery of eight 18-pounders and four howitzers was erected 350 yards from the great wall of the fort, on its south-east side and near the river. In constructing this battery, volunteers from the three British cavalry regiments were employed, and Lake thus secured the European leadership, to which he attached so much importance, without subjecting the 76th to further loss. That regiment was already danger-ously weak, and it was necessary to husband it for the coming fight with the seventeen battalions from the Dec-can. The battery was completed in the course of the day, but the garrison had no head and no heart. They were warned by their deposed officers that, should the fort be stormed, they would be put to the sword, and they now authorised Colonels Hessing and Sutherland to make terms for them.

The intended bombardment was consequently stopped, and in the afternoon of October 13 Captain Salkeld, an officer of General Lake's staff, entered the fort and conveyed the Commander-in-Chief's terms. These demanded the surrender of all treasure, arms, and other munitions of war. The officers and soldiers of the garrison, with their families, were to be free to go wherever they desired. Although the native officers had promised in writing to accept the terms of surrender, whatever they might be, and certainly had no cause for complaint in those offered, Captain Salkeld could obtain no answer. Disputes broke out, and presently the troops on the ramparts opened a furious fire on the British trenches, which continued throughout the night. Salkeld was not injured, but experienced many dangers from friend as well as foe while finding his way back to the British camp. Resistance now appearing inevitable, the cavalry working-parties continued all night in the trenches, but made no answer to the ineffective fire from the ramparts, only firing an occasional shot to drive away the Maratha sharpshooters who, from time to time, approached the very edge of our battery.

Matters continued in this state until October 17, when the battery, having been completed, opened a heavy fire on the south-east bastion of the fort. Two enfilading batteries, placed to either flank of the breaching battery, also came into action, and the fire speedily proved so effective that it was evident that the breach would soon be practicable. The Marathas, on becoming aware of this fact, now determined to abandon the defence, and between five and six thousand men presently marched out and laid down their arms.

Twenty tumbrels laden with treasure, to the amount of

twenty-four *lakhs* of rupees (£250,000), were found in the fort, with 164 guns, ammunition, and stores in abundance.

One of the captured guns, known as "the great gun of Agra," was famous throughout the East. It weighed 30 tons, though the natives believed it to be nearly twice that weight, and was constructed to throw an iron ball weighing 1500 1b. General Lake desired to send this gun as a trophy to the Prince Regent, but when being shipped on a raft on the Jumna the great gun slipped from its lashings and sank into the bed of the river, where it lay until the year 1833, when an economical Governor-General had it burst with gunpowder and the fragments sold by auction—an unromantic method of disposing of an historical relic believed to date from the reign of Akbar. As for the quarter of a million of treasure found at Agra, General Lake followed the ancient custom of our army and at once distributed it as prize-money to the troops. He, as appears from a letter to the Governor-General written on October 22, was uneasy lest this step might not meet with approval, and left his own share of the money untouched until Lord Wellesley's wishes should be known.

The reply of the Governor-General is so cordial in its appreciation of the good qualities of Lake, and so unaffected in its demonstration of brotherly pride in the triumph of Arthur Wellesley at Assaye, that it is worth reading, showing as it does the pleasantest side of Lord Wellesley's character.

Port William
October 29, 1803
My dear Sir,—Your happy success at Agra has afforded me the most cordial satisfaction. This is the fruit of your glory in the field. I have remarked that your humane and generous heart has suffered severely even in the midst of your victories, for the necessary loss of gallant British blood, which must attend

such extraordinary efforts of valour; but I trust you now receive the best consolation for the fall of those whom you have lamented, in reaping the full benefit of their example and noble deeds, and in securing Agra, the most important single object of the war, without effusion of blood, and by the mere lustre and terror of your name. This is the most grateful result of the triumph of our arms; nor can a more convincing proof be afforded of the humane and just policy of that promptitude, decision, and energy which marked your conduct in the commencement of the war. I am persuaded that many lives have been saved by the early sacrifice of a few brave men, whose gallantry has struck terror into the hearts of the enemy. I have considered the fall of Agra as the most propitious event of this wonderful and immortal campaign, and I have received your notification of the surrender of the key of Hindustan as the signal of general rejoicing.

You will have shared my sentiments on the noble and splendid victory gained by my brother on the 23rd of September. His official account of the action has not yet reached me, but I have received authentic accounts of all the particulars of that glorious day, which have been forwarded to you by express; he is worthy to command under your orders; and I should almost have believed that he must have received them from Delhi, before he fought the battle of Assaye. His official return of ordnance taken on the field amounts to ninety-eight pieces of artillery. I have sent you the only official letter yet received from him.

You have now actually accomplished every point of my instructions in the few weeks which have intervened between the 29th of August and the 17th of October. If the successes of your operations stood alone, they would astonish all Asia, but combined with the blows struck in every other quarter, it is impossible to convey to you an adequate idea of the splendour of your fame in this part of the world. With all the sanguine temper of my mind I declare that I could not have hoped for a completion of my plans at once so rapid and so secure. I must now send you fresh instructions, as you have reached the limits of all my first ideas.

You will excuse the delay of my official despatches when you reflect that I am compelled every hour to look all round India, and at this moment endeavouring to despatch to England an adequate representation of your merits and services.

I am particularly anxious to send you an order for the distribution of prize; I hope to be able to furnish it tomorrow. In the meanwhile, you may assure the army that I will grant all within my power, and even stretch that power to the utmost for their interest.

I shall issue a general order, comprehending your operations from the battle of Delhi to the fall of Agra, on Monday.

Ever, my dear General, yours affectionately, with sincere respect and confidence,

Wellesley

Assaye was indeed, as the letter states, fought as if inspired by Lake himself. There was the same disregard of adverse circumstance, and the same dogged determination to do or die, as were shown at Aligarh, Delhi, and Agra. In his after career the great Duke showed qualities of patience and self-restraint nobler perhaps than the rash courage that won Assaye; but in one respect he, to his last fight at Waterloo, always took Lake as his model, namely, in his fixed habit of going to the critical spot, so that, when there was a reverse to be averted or an advantage to be followed up, the commander was ever ready to meet the emergency himself rather than by deputy.

Lake has often been criticised for his exposure of himself to the chances of war, but the most casual study of the Duke of Wellington's career will show that he acted in precisely the same manner, and, of course, with the happiest results.

In another letter to the Governor-General of about the same date, General Lake expresses his great pleasure at the fact that he had not been obliged to storm Agra, as "from the intricate passages in the fort, and the strong garrison, composed of the most desperate caste of men, we must have lost a number of most valuable lives, particularly Europeans, which cannot be spared." Lake was indeed greatly in want of reinforcements. His fifty days of marching and fighting since crossing the Maratha frontier, his three actions—at Aligarh, before Delhi, and at Agra—had cost him nearly 1000 in killed and wounded, to say nothing of the casualties from sickness; he had in addition been obliged to garrison the three captured fortresses and the town of Muttra; and before him lay a task which must immediately be taken in hand—the destruction of the residue of the Maratha army in Hindustan.

This force, known to consist of seventeen battalions of infantry with a numerous artillery, lay at a distance of some thirty miles from Agra, in the neighbourhood of Bhartpur; and although its leaders had not shown sufficient military instinct to attack Lake's army while engaged in the reduction of Agra, the Commander-in-Chief felt that at any moment they might take the easier course of recapturing Delhi, with its inadequate garrison.

Weak as he was, Lake therefore decided at once to grasp the nettle, and, leaving a weak garrison at Agra, marched on October 27 in the direction of his enemy. He could take with him no more than ten battalions of infantry, but all had now seen war and were of tried valour. Above all, he relied on the remains of the 76th, that "handful of heroes" as he presently described them, and on his three cavalry brigades trained under his own eye, and still with their numbers but little diminished.

Marching rapidly, Lake covered sixteen miles in his first march, encamping at Karauli-ki-serai; but owing to heavy rain, unusual at this time of year, he was detained at this place on the following day, October 28.

The march was resumed on the 29th, and the force encamped north-west of Fatehpur-Sikri, that curious and interesting city. Here Lake, desiring to move yet faster, left his heavy guns and baggage under the escort of two battalions of the 4th Brigade, and on October 30 made a march of twenty miles, moving direct on the enemy's guns, which had been heard bombarding the small town of Khatumbar. The march of October 31 brought the army close to this place but a few hours after the enemy had left it, and Lake determined to make a night march and bring on an immediate action. The consequence of this resolution was the battle of Laswari, one of the most severely, contested victories won by the British army in India.

CHAPTER 2
Laswari

In accordance with his determination, Lake set out at the head of all his cavalry at 11 o'clock on the night of October 31, resolved to engage the Marathas and hold them at the place where he might find them, whatever its nature, until the arrival of his infantry, which he ordered to march at 3 o'clock in the following morning. Lake and his cavalry covered twenty-four miles in a ride through the dark ness of some six hours' duration, and came up with the retreating Maratha army near the village of Laswari at about sunrise on the morning of November 1.

They were now commanded by one of their own officers, Abaji by name, a Maratha whose previous career had shown him to be possessed of great pertinacity of character and of considerable military talent. Abaji had at his disposal seventeen battalions of the best infantry; of Perron's army, known as "the Deccan Invincibles"—fifteen battalions having recently marched up from that region, while the other two had escaped from the battle of Delhi. In addition, the Maratha army possessed 72 guns and between 4000 and 5000 horse. Abaji's intention had been to retire into Mewat, a hilly region to the south-west of Delhi, and Lake's determination to bring on a battle before the Marathas could reach that favourable ground was the cause of his rapid night march and somewhat hazardous division of his forces.

When the British cavalry first came in sight, the Marathas showed signs of confusion, and appeared to purpose continuing their retreat; but either from the knowledge that Lake's infantry and heavy artillery could not be within reach, or from fear of attack by the British cavalry while in the act of retreating, Abaji presently turned at bay and showed no mean skill in taking up a defensive position.

His disposition of his infantry and artillery was not dissimilar to that of Bourquin at the battle of Delhi, for the former, in a long line, rested on the villages of Laswari and Malpur, in which were placed a number of guns, and which provided ready-made defences for the flanks. The remainder of the artillery were disposed along the front of the infantry, and were concealed from view by the long grass.

Laswari, the first of the two villages to be reached by the British cavalry, stood close to the north bank of the Baraki *nala*, a small stream running between high and precipitous banks. The Maratha line of battle lay with its right at Laswari, and consequently with the stream in its right rear. The village of Malpur, on which lay the left of the line, was some 2000 yards distant from Laswari. The Maratha cavalry, which was of inferior quality, was drawn up in rear of Malpur, and took no part in the first phase of the fierce action which was now about to begin.

When General Lake first saw the Maratha army, it was difficult to discern its movements. The hurried assemblage of its horse, artillery, infantry, and baggage caused a cloud of dust through which nothing could for a time be seen. Just above the village of Laswari, too, the stream of the Baraki was intercepted by a dam, in order to provide water for a small canal which flowed eastward from the *nala*. Abaji had ordered this dam to be cut, and the water thus suddenly released flowed over the slightly lower ground over which the British cavalry would have to advance to attack the Marathas.

The dust and the inundation confirmed Lake in his belief that Abaji was still endeavouring to escape, and determined at all costs to prevent the removal of the Maratha guns, he ordered his advanced-guard and the 3rd Cavalry Brigade, which had crossed the *nala*, to advance as rapidly as possible through the newly created swamp, move along the whole Maratha front, and attack Malpur and the left portion of the infantry line. This flank movement would clear the ground for the advance of the 1st Cavalry Brigade, which was ordered to cross the *nala* and attack the village of Laswari and the right portion of the infantry line. The 2nd Cavalry Brigade, which was in rear, was to attack in like manner when ordered to do it so. The advanced-guard (one squadron of the 8th Light Dragoons, commanded by Major Griffiths of the 29th Light Dragoons), and the list Brigade (remainder of the 8th Light Dragoons, 1st and 3rd Native Cavalry), commanded by Colonel T. P. Vandeleur, advanced somewhat slowly at first, in consequence of the, inundation, but afterwards at high speed, ignoring the heavy fire opened upon them by all the Maratha guns, which caused numerous casualties among men and horses. Approaching the Maratha left, this fine brigade, headed by the advanced-guard, charged with such impetuosity as to break clean through the Maratha line and to penetrate into the village of Malpur, where they captured several guns. Colonel Vandeleur, however, did not live to lead this gallant charge. Seeing that the moment of action had arrived, immediately before ordering the charge he had turned to address a few words to his own regiment, the 8th Light Dragoons, which were at the head of his brigade, and urged them in spirited language to bring honour to their standards, pointing at the harp and crown with which they were emblazoned. Vandeleur then placed himself at the head of his beloved regiment, and while in the act of drawing his sword, was shot through the heart by a French artilleryman.

Vandeleur offered too conspicuous a mark to the enemy that day, for while his regiment were mounted on grey Arabs, he himself rode a favourite black charger. Lieut.-Colonel Gordon of the 1st Bengal Cavalry now took command of the 1st Brigade, and led it in its glorious and successful charge through the Maratha position. This was an extraordinary achievement, for the Maratha infantry were thickly posted, and were drawn up behind a deep breastwork, strengthened by all the bullock-carts and other vehicles of their army. The guns, too, arranged as has been described along the front, were united to one another by chains, forming an awkward obstacle to cavalry. The Maratha artillerymen, as was commonly the case with natives of India serving in that arm, showed fine courage and devotion, holding their fire until the British cavalry had arrived within twenty yards of the muzzles of the guns. So strongly was General Lake impressed by the conduct of these brave artillerymen that he subsequently enlisted all their survivors who desired it into the British service. Fighting against so determined and powerful an enemy, and in the teeth of such formidable obstacles, it will be readily imagined that the losses of the advanced-guard and 1st Brigade were very heavy. This was particularly the case with the advanced-guard, the first body of troops to come into action, and a brief extract from the Records of the 8th Hussars brings this portion of the battle of Laswari vividly before us:

> Lieutenant Lindon (commanding the leading troop) received a grape-shot in the knee, and died within twenty-four hours in the arms of his beloved friend, Cornet Burrowes. After Lieutenant Lindon

was wounded, the command of the troop devolved on Lieutenant Willard, but he presently had his arm carried away by a charge of grape while cheering on his men under a destructive fire. Cornet Burrowes next took command, and continued at his post in spite of severe wounds in the face and head, received in single combat with a French artillery officer.

The 8th Light Dragoons had 3 officers, 16 rank and file, and 72 horses killed; and 2 officers, 34 sergeants, rank and file, and 24 horses wounded, in addition to 18 horses missing.

While the 1st Brigade was thus distinguishing itself, the 3rd Brigade, under Colonel Macan, was hurrying to the front to deliver its attack on the right flank of the Marathas. The staff of this brigade consisted of three brothers Macan—Richard, the brigadier, Arthur, brigade-major, and Tom, aide-de-camp; none were touched at Laswari, though none but Lake himself can have been more exposed. Macan's brigade came up at a gallop, making for a point a little clear of the village of Laswari, and charged through the enemy's guns and infantry as gallantly and successfully as the 1st Brigade. Having pierced the line, the Brigade immediately formed up again and charged twice more, backwards and forwards, "with surprising order and effect" through the Marathas. All the guns in this portion of the ground were captured, but there were no means of carrying more than two of them off the field, and the enemy was so strong and his fire so severe that Lake ordered the brigade to retire just as Macan was about to lead on his men to a fourth charge.

Similar orders were given to the 1st Brigade; and the Commander-in-Chief, finding that he was losing men and horses with no adequate result, withdrew all the cavalry from the attack and ordered them to form up between the villages of Sahajpur and Singraka, to await the arrival of the infantry. There was no long delay, for, knowing what was before them, the infantry had strained every nerve to be up in time. Marching at three in the morning, they covered the twenty-four miles to the bank of the Baraki *nala*, near Laswari, by eleven o'clock. It was now evident that the Marathas meant fighting, though on the appearance of our infantry they sent Lake word that they might be willing to surrender their guns on certain conditions. Anxious, if possible, to prevent more loss of life, Lake gave the Marathas an hour in which to offer definite terms, and expressed his readiness to accept the conditions tentatively proposed by them. Knowing, however, from his experience at Agra, that the negotiations would probably break down, he continued preparation for renewing the fight if necessary. The galloper guns were withdrawn from the cavalry regiments and formed into two batteries, and the field guns which had been brought up with the infantry were formed into two more.

After the infantry had eaten some food and rested for a short time, it was formed into two columns and ordered to attack the Maratha right, which had now been withdrawn from Laswari.

Far from surrendering, indeed the Maratha general had employed the hour granted him by General Lake in taking up a new and formidable position. Seeing that there was a danger that the British infantry might approach Laswari under cover of the steep bank of the Baraki *nala*, Abaji had now drawn up his infantry in two lines facing east, at right angles with the *nala*, and with the right of the lines between 300 and 400 yards distant from it. The village of Malpur lay between the two lines, near the left flank, and would therefore furnish a rallying-point on that side; but the right flank of the position was *en fair*. To remedy this defect a very strong body of cavalry was posted close in rear of the right of the second line. The artillery, as usual, was distributed along the front and in the village.

General Lake at once saw that the right flank was his point of attack, and ordered his infantry to advance in open company-column along the *nala* until they should have gained a point whence they could advance against the Maratha right. Lake ordered the leading brigade, on arrival at the desired point, to drive in the enemy's infantry and capture Malpur. Colonel Macan was directed to support the advance of the infantry with the 3rd Cavalry Brigade. The 2nd Cavalry Brigade, under Lieut.-Colonel John Vandeleur, was detached towards the Maratha left, to watch for any opportunity of action that might be afforded by the coming infantry attack, and to fall upon the Marathas should they retreat. The 1st Cavalry Brigade under Lieut.-Colonel Gordon, had lost so heavily in the first phase of the battle that Lake now held it in reserve, determined not to employ it further save as a last resource.

Three of the four batteries, whose composition has been described, were ordered to come at once into action against the vastly superior Maratha artillery—a duty which they most gallantly performed, constantly advancing to closer quarters as the infantry gained ground towards Malpur. The fourth battery followed the 76th Regiment, in order to take the first opportunity of enfilading the Maratha position from the right.

These simple and unconditional orders having been explained to all concerned in the quiet interval so conveniently afforded by the enemy, the right wing of the infantry, headed by Lake and General Ware, promptly moved forward, moving in an open column of companies, and taking advantage of the cover afforded by the inequalities of the ground near the bank of the Baraki *nala*.

To divert attention from their advance the three batteries of light guns opened fire, while Colonel Macan, interpreting his orders to support the infantry in a liberal spirit, moved his British regiment, the 29th Light Dragoons, in file along the bed of the *nala*, close alongside the 76th Regiment, which as usual led the right wing. The advance of the 76th, owing to the cover afforded by broken ground and long grass, was for a short time unseen by the Marathas, but as soon as the British regiment came clearly into view every gun opened on them and quickly caused many casualties in their ranks. The distance to be traversed before an attack could be attempted was about a mile; but undeterred by their losses, and the certainty of the storm that would burst upon them whenever they attempted to form up for attack, the 76th pressed doggedly on, closely followed by the battery and by the leading native battalions of the right wing. These were headed by the five companies of the 16th Native Infantry, under Lieut.-Colonel White, which had done such distinguished service in the capture of Agra. The 16th were followed by the 2nd Battalion 12th, the old *"Lal Pultan"* (red regiment) of Plassy, the first Bengal regiment to wear the colour of England. Their commander at Laswari and throughout the campaign was Major Robert Gregory, a most gallant soldier. After the 12th came the two battalions of the 15th Native Infantry. All showed the greatest possible zeal in pressing forward to support the 76th.

Seeing that the fire of his artillery failed to check the British advance, the Maratha general now threw back the right flank of each of his lines of infantry, thus showing a new front towards the *nala*, the point from which it was evident that he would shortly be attacked. This movement was performed with a steadiness which spoke highly for the training and discipline of the Maratha infantry.

As the 76th approached the Maratha position, the battery which followed it found suitable ground near the *nala* from which to open an enfilading fire on the front line of the Marathas. This proved very effective, but the place selected was unfortunately immediately in front of the narrow space on which the 29th Light Dragoons were crowded together in readiness to assist the 76th. The fire of the Maratha artillery, drawn by the British battery, fell heavily on the 29th, for, although they were screened from the view of the Maratha gunners, shots constantly ploughed through the crowded ranks of the Dragoons with fatal effect. The 29th, however, knowing that it was essential that they should hold their ground, bore their losses stoically Among those killed in this place was Major Griffiths, commanding the regiment, whose services in the first phase of the battle, when in command of the advanced-guard, will be remembered. The command of the 29th now devolved on Captain Wade.

Lake, who as usual was in the thickest of the fight, seeing the severity of the Maratha artillery fire, now determined to attack with his leading troops, rather than expose the 29th and 76th to the further heavy losses that they must have suffered had he waited to deploy his whole infantry force. Under his orders, therefore, the 76th advanced single-handed to the attack, whereupon the Maratha guns opened so terrible a fire of canister on them as to cheek even their advance, which ceased at a point outside the village where a mosque afforded them cover. At the same moment Abaji, who had shown his ability as a commander by the skill with which he had previously changed his front, gave further proof of his ability by a well-timed order to his cavalry to charge the 76th in flank. Had this order been obeyed with spirit, it is not too much to say that the 76th would have been destroyed and Laswari would not have been a British victory. The Maratha cavalry were, fortunately, the weak element in their army. Their charge was feeble, and was easily repulsed by the fire of the 76th. The Maratha horse, however, though checked and driven back, rallied at a short distance and showed some signs of intending to repeat their charge. The situation was still highly critical, and Lake ordered the 29th Light Dragoons to advance along the rear of the 76th, form up beyond them, and break the Maratha infantry.

So unfavourable was the ground that the 29th were still compelled to move in file; but in no way daunted, they dashed forward in the most spirited manner and formed up on the left of the 76th. As they came up the Dragoons were heartily cheered by the men of the 76th, and the 29th as heartily cheered in response. Rapidly forming line, the 29th charged without the delay of a moment, and broke through both lines of the Marathas.

The Native Infantry regiments of the right wing were now coming up, and the two leading battalions quickly forming line, were led forward by Lake to reinforce the 76th, and with them follow up the advantage gained by the charge of the 29th. The crisis was, however, still acute, the Marathas standing valiantly to their guns, pouring a concentrated artillery and infantry fire on the two battalions, and facing their charge, bayonet to bayonet. During the single-handed rush of the 76th there had been many casualties both in that regiment and among the headquarter staff. Major-General Ware was dead, his head having been carried off by a round-shot; Campbell and Duval, two of Lake's staff, had also been killed; Colonel Macdonald had been severely wounded, but remained in action, and took General Ware's place during the rest of the day. Lake himself had his charger killed under him, and George Lake was dangerously wounded by a round-shot while giving his own horse to his father.

Not a moment was to be lost. Lake was instantly in the

saddle, and leaving his son apparently dying on the ground, galloped back to the 12th Native Infantry, steadily yet quickly coming forward under their gallant commanding officer, and led them up on the right of the 76th; then, returning once more, he in like manner brought the 16th Native Infantry also into line.

Cheered on by Lake, Macdonald, White, M'Leod, Gregory, and their other officers, the wing hurled themselves against the Marathas, burst through the gaps in their lines made by the charge of the 29th, and attacked the village of Malpur with a fury that none could resist. Meanwhile the 29th Light Dragoons, turning on the Maratha horse, drove them clean off the field, and then, quickly returning, fell upon the rear of the infantry, thus rendering essential aid to the British attack.

The struggle in and around Malpur lasted until four o'clock in the afternoon, by which time all the Maratha guns had been taken, and the right wing of their infantry had been destroyed almost to a man. The left wing preserved its formation throughout this long trial, and seeing that the day was lost, now endeavoured to retreat in good order. This movement gave the desired opportunity to Colonel John Vandeleur and the 2nd Cavalry Brigade, who broke into the Maratha column and captured 2000 prisoners and all the baggage of their army.

Abaji, the commander-in-chief, whose dispositions had been so able throughout the day, now exchanged for a swift horse the elephant on which, according to the custom of Indian armies, he had been mounted, and was thus enabled to escape from the exhausted British cavalry. His name appears no more in history. The destruction of his army was practically complete, for the carnage about Malpur had been terrible. The total of the Maratha losses was never known, but the dead and severely wounded left on the field, most of whom perished there, were estimated at not less than 7000 men. The army created by De Boigne and Perron was defeated but not disgraced; indeed, to have fought as bravely and doggedly as they did, against Lake's heroic troops under his brilliant leadership, reflected the highest honour on the Marathas. No one realised their quality more fully than Lake himself; and Skinner states in his *Memoirs* that when, at the end of the battle, Lake was cheered by his troops, he "took off his hat and thanked them, but told them to despise Death, as those brave fellows had done, pointing to the Marathas who were lying thick about their guns."

In achieving their triumph, the British army sustained very heavy losses. The killed and wounded numbered 822, out of a total force on the ground of about 8000 men. In the 76th Regiment and the Native Infantry of the right wing, who bore the brunt of the second phase of the battle, the losses were very heavy indeed. The British cavalry regiments also suffered severely. The casualties in the 8th Light Dragoons have already been mentioned, and the 29th suffered yet more heavily, losing 19 killed, 5 of whom were officers, and 43 wounded, of whom 3 were officers. The 27th Light Dragoons, though only employed in the last phase of the battle, came off but little more easily. The casualties among horses were extraordinarily heavy, 277 being killed, 154 wounded, and 122 missing.

The physical endurance shown by Lake's army at Laswari deserves record. The cavalry, after marching forty-two miles in less than twenty-four hours, were so hotly engaged from sunrise to sunset that the horses could not be watered or fed for twenty hours. Yet more remarkable was the achievement of the infantry, who went into action after covering sixty-five miles in forty-eight hours.

General Lake's personal share in this bloody struggle was a remarkable one. In the first phase of the battle he shared the dangers of the cavalry, and in the second phase he headed the 76th in their advance and in every charge made by them in the long-sustained fight at close quarters about Malpur. He also successively headed the 12th and 16th Native Infantry, the two regiments that came so staunchly to the assistance of the 76th at a moment when the issue of the battle trembled in the balance. During the critical period when the 29th Light Dragoons were forming at a gallop on the left of the 76th, prior to the attack on Malpur, Lake's horse, Old Port, the gift of Lord Wellesley, which had received several wounds, fell dead under him. His gallant son, Major George Lake, as at the battle of Delhi, at once dismounted and gave up his own charger to his father. Lake at first refused this offer, fearing from the proximity of the enemy that his son's self-sacrifice might cost him his life. After some entreaty the General accepted the horse, and Major Lake, obtaining another mount, was soon again in the saddle. At this moment George Lake was severely wounded by a round-shot, and his father was compelled to leave him lying on the ground, hardly expecting again to see him living.

General Lake, among numberless escapes, was fired at by a Maratha sepoy, who actually placed the muzzle of his firelock against the General's side as he fired. Lake's life was, however, saved by his accidentally turning in another direction, for he had not seen his assailant. His escape was so narrow that his coat was burnt by the explosion of the charge.

At Laswari, however, Lake showed himself much more than a mere fighting general. In this battle he showed, perhaps more conspicuously than on any other occasion in his long career, his qualities as a leader of men. At Laswari were fully displayed his calmness in danger, his self-reliance, and his power of commanding the confidence of his troops. If the narrative of this desperate struggle has conveyed any true idea of its nature to the reader, he will have understood the remarkable qualities of Lake, which carried him triumphantly over obstacles that no other English soldier of the period, save Arthur Wellesley, could have surmounted. It was with reference to Laswari that Malleson wrote of Lake:

> He was never so great as on the battle-field. He could think more clearly under the roar of battle than in the calmness and quiet of his tent. In this respect he resembled Clive. It was this quality which enabled him to dare the almost impossible. That which in others would have been rash, in Lake was prudent daring.

Laswari was the turning-point of the campaign against Sindhia and his allies. Assaye had already been fought and had ruined the hopes of the Maratha confederacy in the south, but Sindhia was still paramount in the vast countries north of the Vindhayan range until the decisive defeat of his sole remaining army at Laswari shattered his power. Twenty days later Argaum was fought by Arthur Wellesley; but that action was a mere rout, and the Maratha troops engaged in it were defeated before they fought. Laswari had taken the fighting stuff out of every man in the Maratha dominions. It was one of the decisive battles of India, and it decided the course of the Maratha War.

The losses among officers were, as usual, abnormally heavy, in Lake's staff alone two being killed and four wounded. Captain Thorn's casualty roll, which is incomplete, gives the names of 15 officers killed and 26 wounded.

The highest in rank of those who fell, Major-General Ware was sixty years of age, and had served forty-one years in India. He was a brave officer, who had frequently distinguished himself in action, and he had been wounded at the battle of Delhi. The story is told that, early in life, Ware had saved a sum of money, which was embezzled by a treacherous friend to whom he had remitted it. Ware thereupon vowed that he would never save another penny, and acted up to his word. He was considered the most hospitable man in Bengal.

As regards the distribution of losses in the infantry, the 76th held a sad pre-eminence. Their casualties numbered 170, of whom 43, including 2 officers, were killed. Of the Native Infantry, the 2nd Battalion 12th sustained 101 casualties, and the six companies of the 16th had no less than 87. They were the two first regiments to come up to the assistance of the 76th, and the conduct of both was admirable. Major Gregory, who led his battalion in fine style, was severely wounded in the head and had his horse shot under him, and Lieut.-Colonel White was also wounded at the head of the 16th.

The foregoing account of the battle of Laswari is based to so considerable an extent on Lake's despatch and letter announcing his victory to the Governor-General, that, to avoid repetition, those passages from them alone follow in which the Commander-in-Chief awards special distinction to corps or individuals. With regard to the first phase of the battle, General Lake offered his "best thanks and acknowledgments" to all the cavalry for the intrepidity and courage displayed. Lieutenants Wallace and Dickson, and the men who served under them with the galloper guns, are selected for special praise. In the second phase, Colonel Macan and his brigade, consisting of the 29th Light Dragoons and 4th Native Cavalry, receive an expression of the Commander-in-Chief's warmest thanks and gratitude for their conspicuous gallantry, Colonel Macan, Captain Wade, and Captain Elliot of this the 3rd Brigade alone being mentioned by name. General Lake also deplores the death of Colonel Vandeleur, "a most valued officer." Of the infantry, Major M'Leod, Captain Robertson, and the officers and men of the 76th Regiment are thanked in similar terms, General Lake in his despatch speaking of the regiment as a "handful of heroes," and adding this glowing testimony to their conduct: "On this, as on every former occasion, His Excellency beheld with admiration the heroic behaviour of the 76th Regiment, whose gallantry must ever leave a lasting impression of gratitude on his mind." Of the Native Infantry, the detachment of the 16th Regiment and the 2nd Battalion 12th are singled out for thanks "for their timely and gallant support of the 76th." The officers mentioned by name are Colonel Macdonald, Lieut.-Colonel White, and Major Gregory.

General Lake again follows his rule of thanking his staff as a body, saying that their zeal at Laswari was but too plainly shown by the returns of killed and wounded. The only officers of the staff mentioned by name were Major-General Ware ("a gallant officer, and one whose loss deeply lament"), Major William Campbell, Deputy Quartermaster-General, and Lieutenant Duval, 19th Light Dragoons, aide-de-camp, all of whom were killed. In conveying General Lake's thanks to the cavalry, Colonel Macan added an honourable mention by himself of Surgeons Lyss and Newman, of the 29th Light Dragoons, for their services to the wounded at the greatest personal risk to themselves.

The night following the battle of Laswari was a very trying one to the exhausted troops. The plain on which the army lay was thickly covered with the bodies of the dead, and on all sides could be heard the groans of the wounded and dying, for whose assistance but scanty resources were at hand. From time to time the air was rent by loud explosions as the flames from the burning village of Malpur caught powder-magazines and tumbrels of ammunition. To crown the sufferings of the troops, a furious hurricane came on at night.

On the following morning (November 2) General Lake, though still much exhausted and depressed after his violent exertions of the previous day, and on account of his anxiety on behalf of his son, wrote the following interesting letter to Lord Wellesley, which gives a vivid picture of the remarkable efficiency of the Maratha army which he had been able to destroy.

Marked Secret
Camp, Laswari
November 2, 1803
I sent you last night an account of our having at length completed the defeat of all the force belonging to Perron or Scindiah on this side of India, which has been effected by great fatigue, difficulty, and severe loss. However, it was an object of such importance to destroy these battalions effectually that I felt it incumbent upon me to use every exertion in my power. . . . Had it been delayed one hour longer they would have escaped entirely. . . . These battalions were most uncommonly well appointed, had a most numerous artillery, as well served as they can possibly be, the gunners standing to their guns until killed by the bayonet. All the sepoys of the enemy behaved exceedingly well, and if they had been commanded by French officers the event would have been, I fear, extremely doubtful. I never was in so severe a business in my life or anything like it, and pray to God I never may be in such a situation again. Their army is better appointed than ours—no expense is spared whatever. They have three times the number of men to a gun we have; their bullocks, of which they have many more than we have, are of a very superior sort; all their men's knapsacks and baggage are carried upon camels, by which means they can

march double the distance. We have taken all their bazaar, baggage, and everything belonging to them; an amazing number of them were killed—indeed the victory has been decisive. The action of yesterday has convinced me how impossible it is to do anything without British troops, and of them there ought to be a very great proportion. The returns of yesterday will, I fear, prove the necessity of what I say too fully. I could not write you, my dear lord, the various occurrences of the week—the wound of my dear son rendered me totally unfit for anything; but I thank God his wound is less severe than I at first believed. When I first saw him upon receiving it, it almost unmanned me, but the alarming crisis when it happened obliged me to quit him and look to the troops, who at that time wanted every assistance I could give them. We fortunately succeeded in carrying our point, by which means I think we shall have destroyed all the force that can now oppose us. I think, without exception, yesterday was the most anxious day I ever experienced, for had we been beaten by these brigades the consequences attending such a defeat must have been most fatal. These fellows fought like devils, or rather heroes, and had we not made a disposition to attack in a style that we should have done against the most formidable army we could have been opposed to, I verily believe, from the position they had taken, might have failed. As it is, I feel happy in having accomplished all your wishes, except Gwalior, which I trust we shall get possession of by treaty with Ambajee. The fall of these brigades will bring him to terms immediately, and will have an effect upon all the different Rajahs who have been looking very much to the proceedings of them, and I suspect many were encouraging them to stand out for some time, and gave them hopes of assistance if they did not absolutely give it them.

I feel great satisfaction that my son is going on well, has no fever, and no doubt of his having the use of his knee. I fear it will be impossible for me to send this evening a detailed account of the action, but hope to be able to send it off tomorrow very early.

I do not think it will be possible for me to move from hence before the 5th on account of my wounded men, and other circumstances; I shall then turn towards Gwalior, in order to arrange matters with Ambajee. I will let you know more of my motions instantly, and remain ever, my dear lord, with unfeigned and sincere attachment, your devoted servant,

G. Lake

General Lake's anticipation of being able to march on November 5 was not fulfilled. He found that the destruction of the Maratha army was even more complete than he had thought, and that there was not anywhere in the field against him a formed body of troops. In these circumstances he was enabled to halt at Laswari until November 8, by which time the air had become unfit to breathe from the great number of dead bodies of men and animals lying about.

The army then marched in a leisurely manner towards Pahesar, a village thirteen miles west of Bhartpur, arriving there on November 14. Here a halt of twelve days was made, and the sick and wounded, together with 71 of the guns captured at Laswari, were sent to Agra. In addition to the guns, the trophies included 44 stand of colours and 5000 stand of arms. The victory had, as Lake anticipated in his letter to the Governor-General, an immediate effect on the native princes of Hindustan. The adhesion of the Raja of Bhartpur has already been recorded. During the halt at Pahesar treaties were concluded with the Rajas of Alwar, Jaipur, and Jodhpur, powerful Rajput chiefs, and with the Begum Sumru, a lady who during the great anarchy in Hindustan, now drawing to its close, had risen from the status of a dancing-girl to that of a ruling chief, owning a small but highly efficient army.

There is a well-known story that, on the arrival of the Begum in the British camp, Lake, who was dining with his staff, and may perhaps have had a glass of the "exhilarating shiraz," received her with a hearty embrace. The Begum, with great tact, turned to her attendants and said, "It is the greeting of a Padre to his daughter!"

On November 27 the army marched to Halena on the Banganga, and there received some welcome reinforcements of Europeans. These consisted of the flank companies of the 1st Bengal European Regiment, and those men of the three British cavalry regiments who had been invalided to Cawnpore and Agra during the campaign from wounds or sickness. There were now with the army a large number of dragoons for whom there were no horses, and they were formed into a temporary battalion of infantry, under the command of Lieut.-Colonel M'Leod of the 76th. The army halted at Halena until December 7, during which period General Lake received the following letter of thanks for his services at Laswari:

Barrackpore
November 18, 1803
My dear Sir,—My last private letter was written under the supposition that the fall of Agra had terminated your difficulties and dangers, and finally crowned your honours in this campaign; but your despatch containing the recital of the glorious and most decisive

victory of the 1st of November afforded a new cause of my admiration and gratitude, and has opened a fresh source of honour for you and your army. I certainly expected that the force collected near Agra would give you some trouble, but I was not prepared for an action so splendid, nor for so formidable an opposition. Your judgment in pursuing this force meets my cordial approbation. Your apprehensions for the safety of Delhi were most wise and just; but even if Delhi had been safe, it would have been necessary to destroy this force before you proceeded further to the southward. The action is one of the most brilliant of which I have ever read the relation. Your personal exertions in it surpass all praise, all example, and all honour and glory acquired by any commander of an army whose actions have reached my knowledge. Your safety in the midst of such perils reminds me of Lord Duncan's private account of the battle of Camperdown, in which, describing his own situation in the midst of the general slaughter, he said, "God covered my head in the day of battle." The dreadful and distracting event of your heroic son's wound in your presence in the heat of action, and in the most urgent and critical moment of your own public duty, was such a trial as Heaven has seldom given to human fortitude. The mere emotion of natural affection would have rendered this trial almost insupportable to any parent; but in addition to the ties of blood, your son possesses your confidence and respect; in his danger you must have felt at once that you were exposed to the loss of your dearest relation, of your best officer, of the true image of your own courage and military spirit, of him who had been your firmest support in all your recent difficulties and dangers, and in whom you must have contemplated the surest pledge of transmitting to later times a just memorial of your own fame. No scene equal to this trial ever was presented to my imagination, nor do I believe it is to be paralleled in all history. With such parental affection as I know you to possess, and with such just sentiments as you entertain of your son's merits and high promise, I declare to you solemnly that your resolution under such a blow, your instant return to the attack of the enemy, and the alacrity and ardour with which you prosecuted the glorious victory of that day, constituted such a variety of extraordinary and affecting circumstances that I could not command strength of mind to read your letter in public. May you never again be subjected to so excruciating a pang, and may the same Providence (that has suffered your gallant son to be wounded on the field of battle before the eyes of his father, and has rescued him from death, and even from injury, to enhance the joys of his father's triumphs) preserve him to emulate his father's example and to secure a succession of hereditary glory to his family, and of victory and fame to his country.

It is impossible not to suffer severe grief in reading the sad list of the killed and wounded on the 1st of November. The names of Vandeleur and of poor Griffith affected me most in the list of killed, the former on account of his high professional character, and the latter on account of my long acquaintance with him. The loss, however, is not great when compared with the force and artillery opposed to us, and it appears to be of still inferior magnitude when compared with the brilliancy of the action, and with its solid and substantial benefit to the common cause. The impression made by the glory of that day, and above all, my dear sir, I must say, by your conduct in it, surpasses all imagination. I am now employed in despatching Colonel Nicholson, who I hope will be liberated in three or four days. I am highly pleased with him; he takes charge of my despatches, of which I will send copies to you immediately. I write to you by Major-General Fraser, most sincerely congratulating you on this last unexpected and unrivalled success, and hoping that your danger is at an end.

I remain, my dear sir, with the greatest attachment and respect,

Wellesley

P.S.—I grieve for the loss of my poor friend Old Port. I have lately received some fine horses from Arabia, one, if not two, of which I hope will be serviceable to you. I shall immediately endeavour to send one to you. *W.*

This cordial, even affectionate, letter requires no comment. It touched the warm heart of Lake, and elicited the following grateful reply:

Camp, Halenah

December 3, 1803

My dear Lord,—Your letter of the 18th, so full of friendship and affection, added to all the kindness I have already received from you, renders me a complete bank-rapt in words to express the sensations which warm my heart with every tie of attachment and gratitude to you, my dear lord, for the various marks of esteem and confidence so repeatedly manifested towards me, and which nothing but death can ever eradicate from my mind, "Your noble and feeling expressions respecting my son, while they afford me the most lively sensations of veneration and regard, call to my recollection what indeed can never be forgot—the pang I felt at the moment I saw him wounded; and believe me, I feel most truly thankful to the Almighty for sparing his life, and, if possible, still more particularly so for having granted me fortitude sufficient to fulfil at that moment the duties of my station, a moment most critical—so much so, that in the event of any failure the mischief that might have ensued is far beyond all calculation. The 1st of November 1803 will ever remain fresh in my mind for various reasons, which cannot now be enumerated: the loss of so many brave men and worthy officers must ever most sincerely regret, and have only to look up to that Providence with adoration and thanksgiving who, in the midst of our most perilous situation, saved so many of us to relate the tale and offer up our prayers for His mercies vouchsafed unto us.

I have received your letter by General Fraser, whom I was extremely happy to see. The duplicate arrived before him, which I will answer in a day or two.

I am, my dear lord, with the truest affection and regard, your devoted servant,

G. *Lake*

On leaving Halena the army marched in a leisurely manner towards Biana, on the Gumbhir, this place having been chosen as a winter camp as a suitable base from which to guard the Rajput states from an attack, which now appeared possible on the part of Holkar.

It may be mentioned that early in this march Ranjit Singh, the Jat Raja of Bhartpur, of whom more will be heard later, visited General Lake's camp and paid his respects. The Raja, is described by Thorn as an elderly little man, dressed in very plain clothes, but followed by a large number of attendants.

During the march also General Lake received an address

from the officers of the army, expressive of the high respect in which they held him, and requesting his acceptance from them of a service of plate of the value of £4000. The address and present, both of which were customary at the period, were accepted with great pleasure by General Lake, and this episode may be considered as the last connected with the battle of Laswari. The army arrived at Biana on December 27, 1803, and remained there unmolested until February 9 in the following year.

In order to complete the narrative of the campaign of 1803, we must now turn to the operations of the detachment which, it will be remembered, was stationed at the opening of the campaign at Allahabad. This force, under Lieut.-Colonel Peregrine Powell, was intended to invade Bundelkhand and eventually to capture Sindhia's fortresses in that region. Colonel Powell marched from Allahabad, under Lake's orders, on September 6, and after an easy defeat of a force under Shamshir Bahadur, Sindhia's local commander, captured Kalpi on December 4. Shamshir Bahadur then surrendered, and his example was presently followed by the Subadar of Jhansi (ancestor of the Rani of Jhansi who was killed in action in the Indian Mutiny).

Sindhia's officers were now all deserting him, and among the traitors was Ambaji Inglia, who engaged to surrender Gwalior, Sindhia's most important fortress. General Lake consequently detached a force from the main army to take over charge of Gwalior, selecting as its commander Lieut.-Colonel White of the 16th Native Infantry, who was not incapacitated from duty by a grape-shot wound received at Laswari, and, by his services throughout the campaign, had shown himself fitted for an independent command.

White, who was given the rank of Brigadier-General, arrived before Gwalior about December 23, but on summoning the Killadar or fort-commandant to surrender his charge, the latter refused to comply with the orders of Ambaji Inglia. General Lake promptly reinforced White's force, bringing it up to four and a half battalions of Native Infantry, a battalion formed of the flank companies of the 22nd Regiment and the Bengal European Regiment under Major M'Leod of the 76th Regiment, and some heavy guns manned by a company of European artillerymen.

Gwalior was a fortress of immense strength, constructed on a rock which rises abruptly out of the plain to a height of 300 feet. A great part of the perimeter, which has a total length of nearly five miles, is absolutely inaccessible.

Nothing daunted, White at once opened a regular attack on the fortress, and by February 4, 1804, had made a practicable breach in the wall. The garrison then made terms of surrender, and Gwalior was evacuated on February 5. A highly complimentary order was issued on the occasion by General Lake, and it is to be noted that the services of Captain Wood, the senior engineer officer, received special mention.

The capture of Gwalior took place several weeks after the official end of the campaign against Sindhia and the Raja of Berar, for a treaty of peace had been signed by those princes on December 30, 1803. It was, however, already evident that the end of the war was yet far off.

CHAPTER 3

The Campaign Against Holkar

Towards the end of the campaign against Sindhia and the Raja of Berar, it had become clear to Lord Wellesley that Holkar was unlikely to refrain much longer from hostilities.

Holkar had, in fact, been swayed throughout the campaign by two conflicting motives—his desire to overwhelm the British, which impelled him to an alliance with Sindhia and the Bhonsla, and his fear of assisting Sindhia to become the chief power in India. Finally his jealousy and distrust of Sindhia proved stronger than his hatred of the British, and Holkar stood by inactive while Lake and Arthur Wellesley crushed the confederacy which his aid might have rendered too powerful for them.

Laswari and Assaye freed the hands of Lord Wellesley as they never had been free from the day of his assuming the office of Governor-General; yet his two armies were widely separated, and both were much diminished in strength from the arduous campaign then approaching its close, and Holkar judged that the time had come for him to enter the field.

He had, from the position of his dominions, freedom of choice as to his point of attack, and Lake's army being not only much weaker than that of Arthur Wellesley, but easier to cut off from its base, it was against Lake that Holkar decided to move.

One of the first signs of Holkar's definite decision to defy the British was his cruel murder of three Anglo-Indian officers who had done good service for him in past wars, but now refused to serve against their countrymen. After this atrocity Holkar moved northward from Indore, his capital, and threatened the dominions of the Rajput Raja of Jaipur, the hereditary enemy of the Maratha princes, and now a tributary of the British.

In this intention Holkar was frustrated by the movements of Lake, who after the battle of Laswari marched, as has been stated, to Biana, where he was conveniently situated to guard both the Rajput states and the way towards the British frontier. Jaipur being thus denied to him, Holkar returned southward and plundered Mahesar, a rich city on the Narbadda. It is said that he here obtained no less a sum than £1,000,000, and with this treasure at his command, and his army swollen by large numbers of Sindhia's soldiers, both horse and foot, who had flocked to him after the defeat of their master, Holkar determined on war with the British.

His action was absolutely unprovoked. Lord Wellesley had made every effort to avert war, sending as late as February 10, 1804, assurances that Holkar would not be molested so long as he would refrain from attacking the territory of the Company and its allies. Six days later, in reply to an invitation previously sent to Holkar by General Lake, envoys appeared in the Commander-in-Chief's camp, who propounded the Maratha chief's demands. These were obviously inadmissible, including the payment of tribute to him by the Company, cession of territory to which he had no legal claim in the Doab and in Bundelkhand, and a guarantee of the territories actually in his possession, some the property of chiefs under British protection. Holkar further demanded that a treaty similar to that just concluded with Sindhia should be concluded with him. The alternative—war—was preferred in the following terms:

> Friendship requires that, keeping in your view the long-existing unanimity between me and the English Company, you act according to what my *vakeels* (envoys) shall represent to you; if not, my country and property are upon the saddle of my horse; and, please God, to whatever side the reins of the horses of my brave warriors may be turned, the whole of the country in that direction shall come into my possession.

Holkar's envoys spoke in a tone corresponding to that of their master's letter, asserting that Holkar had 150,000 horsemen of his own, in addition to 40,000 Rohillas who had offered to serve him for three years without pay, on condition of being allowed to plunder the Company's territory.

General Lake responded to these threats and demands with becoming brevity, saying that it was not the custom of the English to boast of their power, but that, in the event of war, Holkar would possibly find that he had overestimated his own strength. The utmost moderation was, however, still shown, and Holkar was given yet more chances of coming to terms. Insolent as was his demeanour, Lord Wellesley was most anxious to avoid the necessity of war. Men, horses, supplies, and money were all deficient, and the hot weather was impending. Lake was as anxious as the Governor-General to avert war, and in a private letter wrote to him early in April:

> If Holkar should break into Hindustan he will be joined by the Rohillas. I never was so plagued as I am by this devil. We are obliged to remain in the field at an enormous cost. If we retire he will come down upon Jaipur and exact a *crore* (£1,000,000) from the Raja,

and then pay his army and render it more formidable than ever. If I advance and leave an opening, he will give me the slip, and get into our territories with his horse, and burn and destroy.

Lord Wellesley now became convinced that war could not be averted, and entered into consultation with Lake and Arthur Wellesley as to the best manner of engaging Holkar. Arthur Wellesley was unable to offer a very active co-operation. He was at the head of large force in the Deccan, but there had been a famine in that part of India, and for the moment he could not move. He engaged, however, as soon as rain should have supplied him with grass and grain for his army, to occupy Holkar's possessions in his vicinity. The force in Gujarat, under Colonel Murray, was immediately available, and was now encamped about seventy miles north of Baroda.

Arthur Wellesley therefore suggested that the principal advance should be made from the north by Lake, that Sindhia should be called upon to join in with it and to supply a strong contingent of cavalry, and should also furnish cavalry for Murray, whose force was sufficiently strong in infantry. Thus strengthened, Murray could advance to Indore, while Lake, with the assistance of Sindhia's horse, drove Holkar back from the north. If, however, it was practicable to delay operations until after the rains, Wellesley proposed that he should then enter Hindustan at the head of Murray's force and as much of his own army as could be spared from the Deccan. In this way, he submitted, Holkar could assuredly be crushed.

It must be remembered that the Governor-General, Lake, Arthur Wellesley, and Murray were far apart from one another, and that letters from one to the other often passed through hostile country and sometimes miscarried, and that in all cases communications were slow. Thus it came about that before he had been able to consider the wise proposals of his brother, Lord Wellesley had already instructed General Lake to commence operations against Holkar. At the same time he informed Arthur Wellesley of the fact, and directed him to cooperate with Lake.

These orders were issued in the middle of April 1804, when Lake was in camp some twenty-five miles north-east of Tonk.

Arthur Wellesley, being unable to move from the Deccan, directed Colonel Murray to advance from Gujarat in co-operation with the movements about to be undertaken by Lake; but, as will hereafter be seen, Murray, who was a man of undecided character, made but a short advance, which he converted into a retirement at the moment when his support was most needed.

When Lake received his orders to attack Holkar, the latter had again advanced towards Rajputana, and with a part of his army was threatening the city of Jaipur. Colonel Monson, who had now recovered from the severe wound which he sustained at the storming of Aligarh, had rejoined the army, and on April 18 Lake despatched him, at the head of a detachment of three battalions of infantry, to protect that city. Monson arrived at Jaipur on April 21, whereupon Holkar retired southward. On April 27 Lake also advanced with his main body, and on May 8 was at Nawai, fifteen miles north-east of Tonk.

From this place he despatched a second detachment, consisting of a regiment of cavalry, two battalions of infantry, and some guns, against Rampura, a Rajput town in the possession of Holkar, situated sixty miles south-east of Jaipur. This detachment was commanded by Lieut.-Colonel Patrick Don, an excellent officer of the Bengal army, who had served during the early part of the war in Bundelkhand under Lieut.-Colonel Powell. Don, who had no means of undertaking a regular siege, determined to capture Rampura by a *coup-de-main*, and, to avert suspicion from his design, encamped on the side of the town farthest removed from the principal gateway, which he intended to attack. At 2 a.m. on May 15, Don marched from his camp at the head of eight picked companies of infantry, with one 12-pounder; while a covering party, consisting of three companies with the five remaining guns, followed in rear. The cavalry were left in camp until their services should be required.

Colonel Don and his detachment marched rapidly and silently round the town towards the gateway, making no reply to the ill-aimed fire directed on them from the ramparts. On reaching the gateway Don brought up his 12-pounder and quickly broke down the gate, while his supporting infantry poured an effective fire on the garrison as they crowded the ramparts near the point of attack. Rampura, like Aligarh, was defended by four successive gates. The storming-party found the second gate open, it being out of repair, and the third and fourth were quickly blown in like the first. Don's force now prepared to attack the fort, before the gate of which they had arrived through the town, but the garrison had lost heart and endeavoured to escape. Don's stormers, therefore, forced their way without difficulty through the gateway of the fort and completed the capture. The entire garrison was then driven out of both town and fort, many being cut down by the 3rd Bengal Cavalry, who awaited them outside the walls. The capture of Rampura was a gallant and well-managed affair, and the skill and decision shown by Lieut.-Colonel Don and his detachment were highly eulogised by General Lake.

The loss of Rampura completed the discomfiture of Holkar, who made a further retirement into his territories south of the river Chambal. The heat was now very great, and was severely trying the European portion of Lake's army, who had now been for a considerable time exposed to the weather and showed need of shelter. Holkar was so far removed from regions whence he could threaten British territory that no action on his part appeared probable before the end of the hot weather. Lake saw also that no movement from the north was likely to be effective in bringing Holkar to a decisive action, and that it would be better to wait until after the rains, when a combined operation, as suggested by Arthur Wellesley, would finish off the war.

For all these reasons Lake decided to withdraw his main army to Agra and Cawnpore, placing the Europeans in their barracks at the latter station. As a safeguard against any possible attempt at mischief on the part of Holkar he decided to increase the strength of Monson's detachment to five battalions, and to call upon Sindhia to furnish it with a large contingent of cavalry. With this force, and with the strong post of Rampura behind him, Monson should be able to hold his ground against any force that could be brought against him until the main army was again ready to take the field. Monson unfortunately proved to be an incapable though brave and enterprising commander, and a narrative of the misfortunes of his detachment has a painful interest for us, even after the lapse of a century. Its retreat before Holkar was the first serious military reverse suffered by British arms in India.

The detachment handed over to Monson was of considerable strength, and, as regards the artillery and infantry, of excellent quality. The infantry battalions (2nd Battalion 2nd, 1st and 2nd Battalions 12th, 2nd Battalion 21st, notwithstanding the very short service of the last-named corps) were among the finest in the Bengal army, and were presently joined by the 2nd Battalion 8th from Rampura under their distinguished commanding officer,

Lieut.-Colonel Don. A company of European artillerymen manned the two 12-pounders and ten 6-pounders with the force, and there were in addition six galloper guns to serve with the irregular horse. With these artillerymen was Captain-Lieutenant Wimbolt, the officer whose services at Shikohabad have been mentioned, now released from his obligation not to serve in the field, Sindiah being no longer the enemy.

The weak spot in the detachment was the doubtful quality of a portion of the irregular horse, composed of recently raised irregular corps, and of small contingents from various native states, loosely organised and inadequately trained. The strength of this arm was about 3000 men, under the command of Lieutenant Lucan, 74th Regiment, of whom we have heard so much in the course of this narrative.

Leaving Monson with his detachment near Jaipur, and merely giving him general instructions to guard against any move on the part of Holkar, General Lake started on May 18 for his march of 140 miles to Agra. The heat was now almost unendurable in the open, and the Europeans and natives alike suffered terribly from the hot winds, which can only be compared to the blast of a furnace. Many brave fellows who had survived the battles of Delhi, Agra, and Laswari died in this fearful march. On May 30 nineteen Europeans perished in the four weak regiments with the main army (the three dragoon regiments and the 76th), and an even greater number on June 2. On the latter day no less than 250 camp-followers are said to have died. At last the infantry marched into Agra and found shelter on June 7, and the cavalry arrived at Cawnpore thirteen days later.

No sooner had the main army started on its return march than things began to go wrong with the detachments. The first misfortune occurred early in May in Bundelkhand.

The command there had at first been in the competent hands of Lieut.-Colonel Peregrine Powell, but this officer had fallen into ill-health and had been compelled to hand over his duties.

His successor, Lieut.-Colonel Fawcett, who was in camp at Kunch, sent a detachment of seven companies of Native Infantry, with six guns, to capture the small fort of Bela, about eight miles away. Captain Smith, the officer commanding this small detachment, unwisely subdivided it, and placed two of his companies and five guns in the trenches before Bela, while the remainder of the detachment was in camp, too far distant to support them. The commandant of Bela lulled Captain Smith into carelessness by a pretended surrender, and treacherously invited Amir Khan to come to his rescue. Amir Khan, a famous freebooter of the period, who was at the head of a large force, and was now in the interest of Holkar, fell suddenly upon the unfortunate troops in the trenches before Bela, and put them all to the sword. Captain Smith had no time to come to their rescue, even if he had thought it possible, but succeeded in fighting his way back to Kunch with the remaining five companies and one gun. Lieut.-Colonel Fawcett, instead of marching to attack Amir Khan, whose force, though large, was not formidable, lost his head and retired up the river Betwa, leaving Bundelkhand open to the enemy.

Fawcett was removed from his command, and Amir Khan's troops soon afterwards sustained several reverses at the hands of Fawcett's successor, Lieut.-Colonel Martindell, and his subordinates, but Bundelkhand was not finally subdued until 1809.

The affair at Bela fades, however, into insignificance by the side of Monson's disaster.

That officer, when first left to his own resources, showed complete confidence, and in spite of the great heat evidently intended to exhibit activity and enterprise. He moved southward, presumably on hearing of Murray's abortive advance, and on June 2 was at Kotah, when he was joined by Lieut.-Colonel Don with the 2nd Battalion 8th Native Infantry from Rampura, and by 1500 Maratha horse under a chief named Bapuji Sindhia.

Monson now considered himself strong enough to enter Holkar's territory, and marched through the Mokandara Pass and on to the town of Sonara. On July 2 he captured by escalade the strong fort of Hinglazgarh—a gallant enterprise executed in Monson's best style. The fort was captured by the 2nd Battalion 2nd Native Infantry, led by their brave commanding officer, Major Sinclair, and by Monson himself. Sinclair and his battalion remained in garrison at Hinglazgarh, and Monson rejoined his main body. So far all had gone well with him, though he had latterly experienced difficulty as to supplies, and the commencement of the rains was making marching more and more difficult. Now, however, his troubles were to begin, for he simultaneously heard that Colonel Murray, instead of advancing from Gujarat to join hands with him, was falling back, while Holkar in great strength was on the Chambal within forty miles of his camp. Monson was now in a most critical position, and had to make an immediate choice between an attack on the vastly superior force of Holkar and a difficult and dangerous retirement. Monson's full reasons for not fighting are unknown, for it does not appear that he was ever called upon to state them, but he elected to retire. His high courage would certainly have led him to attack Holkar, had he thought it possible to bring him to decisive action, and he probably thought that after a running fight with Holkar's force, which was more mobile and fresher than his own, he would still have been compelled to retreat, and would have been in even worse condition to do so.

Monson's retreat began on July 8, on which date his camp was distant thirty miles from the Mokandara Pass, and about double that distance from Kotah. At four in the morning Monson despatched his baggage and stores towards Sonara, the halting-place between his position and the pass, and kept his force formed up and ready for action until eleven o'clock, anticipating an attack by Holkar.

None came; so Monson, ordering his mounted troops under Lucan and Bapuji Sindhia to follow him half an hour later, marched off northward after his baggage. Monson's troops then marched nine miles, but saw no more of their cavalry, nor did Monson learn for some time why Lucan had failed to carry out his orders to follow him. Some time before Monson reached Sonara, however, Bapuji Sindhia rode up unattended and informed him that the cavalry had been attacked and defeated with heavy loss, and that Lucan was wounded and a prisoner. Bapuji, who was a traitor, subsequently made his escape and openly joined Holkar, who gave him a large command.

James Skinner, who had the best means of ascertaining what happened to the unfortunate Lucan and his cavalry, states in his memoirs that the disaster was thus brought about. Lucan had under him nearly 5000 men, with six guns. He was extremely anxious to distinguish himself in the British service, and when Holkar's advanced-guard appeared on the scene soon after Monson had marched off, decided to try the effect of a bold charge. This might well have succeeded had Lucan's troops all remained staunch, but Bapuji Sindhia's men at once deserted him and joined Holkar's troops. This large defection proved fatal. Lucan's own men fought bravely, as did two corps of 500 men each commanded by a Rajput prince. Lucan, though wounded early in the fight, made a brave resistance, but was finally overcome and captured. A great number of his men and of the Rajputs, together with their brave and loyal chiefs, were put to the sword, and the remainder dispersed. The unfortunate Lucan was never seen again. He perished at the hand of the savage Holkar, either from his wounds or by torture or poison.

Monson arrived at Sonara at 9 p.m., after a march of nearly thirty miles. A little later Major Sinclair arrived with his battalion (the 2nd of the 2nd Native Infantry) from Hinglazgarh, where, it will be remembered, he had been left in garrison. Sinclair left one company at Hinglazgarh under Lieutenant Owen, who was joined by a Lieutenant Davidson, who had missed his way while proceeding to join his regiment with a convoy of ammunition. These two officers were, it is stated, soon afterwards betrayed to Holkar, and were beheaded by order of Harnat Singh, an adopted son of Holkar, at the Bundi Pass. The garrison of Hinglazgarh and Davidson's party entered Holkar's service under compulsion.

Monson continued his retreat from Sonara on July 9, and reached the Mokandara Pass at noon unmolested. This was in itself a strong position, but liable to be turned by way of another pass some eight or nine miles distant. Monson therefore decided to continue his march. The southern entrance of the Pass was fortified by a strong gateway, with a loopholed parapet ascending the hill on either side. Lieut.-Colonel Don was ordered to hold this gateway with his regiment while the rest of the column continued its retreat through the pass. This duty Don performed well, assisted by Captain Fetherston, who, with two companies of the 12th Native Infantry, guarded a ford across a *nala* in front of the Pass.

It was night when Lieut.-Colonel Don commenced to move off his ground. The frequent flashes of lightning were at times the only guide along the rugged path, now converted into a rushing torrent. Having cleared his position, Don blocked the gateway with heavy stones. A *havildar* sent to recall Fetherston reported that he had already retired; but Don knew that Fetherston would never have left his post without orders, and sent a second and more trustworthy messenger. The gateway was now securely blocked, and at 2 a.m. on July 10 Don began to traverse the defile. It was intensely dark: the guns had to be dragged over rocks with infinite labour by the light of portfires, 500 of which the artillerymen expended before morning. The retreat continued through the following day, and early on July 12 the force arrived at Kotah. Here Colonel Monson desired to purchase supplies and to leave two 12-pounders in charge of the Raja, as the gun-bullocks had suffered much from the heavy condition of the ground. The Raja, however, not unreasonably refused to accept the guns, pleading that as Monson intended to leave Kotah, he would merely incur the wrath of Holkar and be unable to preserve the guns from capture.

Monson left Kotah on July 13, but the country was now so boggy that his force could only reach the Gamach Ghat (ford), on the Chambal river, seven miles away. The river was unfordable on the arrival of the detachment at the Ghat, and although a crossing was effected on the 14th, a halt was found necessary for the purpose of collecting supplies.

Monson was ready to march on July 15, but the rains rendered it impossible to move the guns: no provisions remained, and the only course was to spike and abandon the guns. This was done at daybreak on the following morning, and the ammunition was destroyed. The march which followed was of a terrible nature, and the sufferings of the troops can only be estimated by those acquainted with the rains of India. During the day no less than fifteen elephants and a large number of camels were left actually embedded in the mud, and it is recorded that only one small tent was pitched that evening in the whole detachment.

The march performed on July 17 was of a similar nature, and all the food eaten by the troops was a little wheat procured from a small village. The European officers and gunners bought and killed a wretched bullock from the same village, which they cooked as best they could. In the afternoon the force arrived at the Mej river, a small stream which was now found to be 300 feet across and 6 feet deep. On the previous day Lieut. Dalton of the 12th Native Infantry, who had lost a leg at the battle of Laswari, had been drowned at this place, which he had reached on his way to rejoin his regiment.

None of the detachment were able to cross the Mej on July 18 except the European artillerymen, who were ordered by Colonel Monson to cross on their remaining elephants and proceed to Rampura. The remainder of the detachment were compelled to remain where they were for eight days, but Holkar was evidently unable to take advantage of this favourable opportunity. A party of 500 of his horse arrived on July 23 within eight miles of Monson's camping-ground, and Monson at once attacked them. The force sent against them consisted of all the flank companies of the detachment, commanded by Captain O'Donnell. This officer divided his force into three parties, and having surrounded the Maratha camp under cover of heavy rain, charged in and dispersed the horsemen, killing forty or fifty of them and capturing many horses and camels. This, in the trying circumstances, was a most dashing feat of arms, and for a time greatly raised the spirits of the detachment.

On July 25 the water in the Mej had fallen considerably, but it was not yet fordable. On the 26th the 2nd Battalion 21st crossed on five elephants, followed by the 2nd Battalion 12th. When half the latter corps had crossed, the Maratha horse began to threaten the troops remaining on the south bank. At first a small number showed, but by 3 p.m. about 2000 Marathas had closed up to the outpost line. They, however, showed little enterprise and withdrew at dusk, and the whole detachment succeeded in crossing in the course of July 27. There had, however, been a great loss of life among the unfortunate camp-followers, numbers of whom were drowned while crossing the Mej on small and unstable rafts.

Within a short distance of the Mej was the mouth of the Lakeri Pass, through which the detachment continued its retirement to Rampura. There was no organised attack, but all stragglers from the battalions and a great number of camp-followers were murdered by Minahs, a predatory tribe.

Rampura lay eighteen miles beyond the northern outlet of the Lakeri Pass, and the whole force had arrived at that town by July 30 and encamped on the glacis of the fort, erecting any poor shelters obtainable. Colonel Monson, who had arrived at Rampura with the 2nd Battalion 2nd Native Infantry four or five days earlier, had busied himself with some slight success in collecting supplies. He here received orders from General Lake not to fall back beyond Kotah; but that place was forty-five miles behind him, and it was impossible for him to retrace his footsteps. From various letters written by Monson at this time, it is evident that his misfortunes had been too much for his endurance. He incessantly changed his plans, and issued orders one day only to cancel them the next.

On August 14 reinforcements arrived from Agra, consisting of the 2nd Battalion 9th Native Infantry and the 1st Battalion 14th Native Infantry, under Lieut.-Colonels M'Culloch and Ashe—two fine battalions, well commanded; also a body of irregular horse, quite untrustworthy, and six guns. The detachment was now stronger than ever; but unfortunately the reinforcements brought but scanty supplies with them, and their arrival therefore made it more difficult for Monson to hold his ground.

Holkar's army now approached Rampura in two large bodies—one commanded by himself, and the second by the traitor Bapuji Sindhia. Monson finally decided to continue his retreat, leaving a garrison of one battalion and four companies with four guns in the fort of Rampura. The battalion selected was the 2nd Battalion 8th Native Infantry, but Lieut.-Colonel Don was too ill from privations and exposure to remain with it, and accompanied the main body as an invalid.

This force, now consisting of five and a half battalions—2nd Battalion 2nd, 1st Battalion 9th, 1st Battalion 14th, lst and 2nd Battalions 12th, and six companies 21st Native Infantry, the remainder of the 21st were left at Rampura—with two howitzers, marched from Rampura on August 21 in the direction of Khushalgarh, but on the following day, soon after sunrise, was stopped by the Banas river twenty miles away. Holkar showed himself as incompetent a general as Monson, and had made no dispositions to forbid the crossing; but Monson also had lost the opportunity given him by his long halt at Rampura of collecting boats and securing the crossing-place, and this neglect proved the ruin of his unfortunate force.

On August 23 three small boats were obtained, in which the treasure of its detachment, with its escort of six companies 21st Native Infantry, and the sick and wounded of the detachment, were ferried across. These details, under Captain William Nicholl, the commanding officer of the 21st Native Infantry, had written orders to proceed at once to the mud fort of Baroda, eighteen miles on the way to Khushalgarh. On arriving at Baroda, Captain Nicholl, an experienced officer of twenty-three years' service, found the position so weak that, on his own responsibility, he disobeyed his orders and pushed on to Khushalgarh. By this independent conduct, and by his subsequent admirable behaviour at Khushalgarh, Captain Nicholl saved Monson's force from destruction or capture at that place.

On the 24th the Banas had fallen and was fordable. Three battalions crossed by wading, carrying their arms and accoutrements on their heads—the rear-guard, consisting of the 2nd Battalion 2nd Native Infantry and a company of the 9th Native Infantry, holding the south bank to cover the crossing of the baggage and camp-followers.

Major Sinclair presently found that the Marathas had surrounded the rear-guard at such close range that it would be impossible for him to cross the river. He therefore, at the head of his own battalion and of the picquets of the 9th Native Infantry, made a gallant charge, capturing eleven of the Maratha guns and driving the enemy from them. Sinclair himself, a man of slight frame and in bad health, planted with his own hand the colour of his regiment in the Maratha battery, but at this moment he was wounded in the knee and fell to the ground. Seeing his fall, the Marathas rallied, charged the rear-guard sword in hand, broke them, and drove them into the river. Sinclair and twelve other officers were killed.

Colonel Monson, who had remained with the rear-guard and had shown his unfailing personal courage throughout the struggle, was wounded and hardly escaped. The only survivor of the officers of the 2nd Battalion 2nd Native Infantry was a lieutenant who had been wounded and carried off the field early in the day. The picquets of the 9th Native Infantry were killed or drowned to a man, and but few of the brave 2nd, all of them wounded, made their way across the river. A native officer was seen carrying the colours of the regiment in one hand and defending himself with the other, but he fell in mid-stream, and he and the colours were seen no more. One of the two howitzers with the force was captured in consequence of the destruction of the rear-guard, and the greater part of the baggage also fell into the hands of the enemy. The original detachment had nothing to lose, and the 9th and 14th, which had joined at Rampura, were now equally destitute.

The detachment moved on from the Banas river at seven in the evening, formed in a hollow square, with the howitzer, the remaining baggage, and the surviving camp-followers in the centre. The enemy's horse accompanied them, and made many attempts to charge the rear-face. At about 11 p.m. a horseman galloped up to the square. His horse was shot and he fell to the earth, stunned and slightly wounded. He proved to be Lieutenant Shaw of the 14th Native Infantry, who, in consequence of a previous wound, had been placed on a camel, and had so fallen into the hands of the enemy. The Marathas had put him on a pony, and he had taken this opportunity to escape.

The detachment continued its retreat on August 25, and though harassed until six in the evening by the enemy's horse, the corps kept their discipline and formation, and repulsed all attacks. The fire of the howitzer proved most valuable this day. At seven o'clock the detachment had the good fortune to meet a Brinjari convoy of 1000 bullocks carrying grain, which had been sent from Agra, and by some accident had not discovered the troops at Khushalgarh. This was a godsend, for the sepoys had had no food for two days. After an uncooked meal the exhausted detachment struggled into Khushalgarh, having marched thirty-six miles in thirty hours.

Here Monson had expected to be reinforced by a considerable body of Sindhia's troops with twenty-five guns. On hearing of Monson's misfortunes, however, the Maratha officer in command showed open hostility, and called on Captain Nicholl to deliver to him the treasure which he had brought from the Banas river. Nicholl showed so bold a front that, after two faint-hearted attacks, the Marathas withdrew. Soon afterwards Monson arrived with his exhausted troops. Had Captain Nicholl failed to hold Khushalgarh, Monson's force would have had no place of refuge.

On the following day, August 26, Monson ordered a halt, and the grain was served out.

Until this date the conduct of the detachment had been admirable, but now, unhappily, symptoms of disaffection appeared in the 9th and 14th Regiments, who refused to accept their rations, saying that they would rather have nothing than hard grain. In justice to the sepoys, it must be added that seldom had troops been more severely tried. So long-continued a retreat was calculated to try the moral of any troops, and every mode of bribery had been constantly tried by the enemy. Money was offered, promotion was held out to all who would desert their colours and give up their officers, and the most cruel death threatened to those who might refuse these offers and afterwards fall into the enemy's hands. In spite of all these temptations and their great sufferings, the 12th and other regiments remained loyal almost to a man, and the desertions from the 9th and 14th Regiments were not wholesale. The total number of those who deserted is unknown, and is stated variously at two to five companies in the entire detachment.

During the halt the Marathas collected round Khushalgarh in great numbers, estimated at 20,000 horse, with some infantry battalions and twenty-five guns. The town was completely surrounded, but at dusk the enemy withdrew some distance.

At 8 p.m. Monson silently evacuated the town, and when outside the gateway reformed his square and continued his retreat. The enemy constantly charged the rear of the square, but were always repulsed by the brave and steady 2nd Battalion 21st Native Infantry, the only corps of young soldiers in the detachment, not a man of whom (except the sergeants) was more than twenty-three years of age. These attacks continued until noon on August 27, when the Marathas drew off; but it was now found necessary to spike and abandon the last-remaining howitzer, the bullocks being no longer able to drag it. The weary troops continued their march until sunset, when they arrived at Hindun. The enemy held the town, but a ruined fort near the town was found unoccupied and seized. No long halt was possible, and Monson determined to give the troops a few hours' rest and to march about midnight.

The detachment moved out of the ruined fort at one o'clock in the morning of August 28, and formed square as before. At 6 a.m. some ravines were entered, and the square did not clear them for an hour. This was a fatiguing operation, and caused some straggling. Just as the square left the broken ground in somewhat loose order, a desperate charge was made on it by the Maratha horse in three strong bodies. Fatigue was forgotten, discipline rose triumphant, and the square was ready in good time.

The sepoys, obedient to the orders of the few remaining officers, held their fire until the Marathas were within fifty yards of the right face of the square. This was formed of the 12th and 21st Regiments, who now opened a steady file-firing, almost every shot taking effect from the great numbers of the enemy. The Marathas lost heavily, and retired in disorder. Their chiefs endeavoured to bring them to the charge again, but without success. Instead of charging they opened a heavy fire, which caused many casualties. The square now moved on, but were unhappily obliged to leave many of their wounded on the ground, who were all cruelly murdered. This repulse of the Maratha horse was the last triumph of the unfortunate detachment.

At sunset the force reached the Biana Pass, where on account of the exhausted and Buffering condition of the troops Monson halted and would have passed the night; but the enemy brought up his guns and opened so galling a fire that Monson was obliged to continue his retreat, which was continued to the town of Biana. But the night was dark, the camp-followers and baggage got mixed with the line, the troops were thrown into inextricable confusion, order could no more be restored, the troops fairly broke and fled; and such as escaped the straggling parties of the enemy—for there was no further regular attack—made their way to Agra, which they reached in flying and detached groups on August 31.

With these words James Skinner concludes his narrative of Monson's terrible retreat, which, in conjunction with the very clear and straightforward despatch of the latter, gives the most intelligible account of the disaster. It is estimated that between 300 and 400 survivors of each battalion, except the 2nd Battalion 2nd Regiment, whose destruction has been mentioned, eventually reached Agra. Lieut.-Colonel St George Ashe, of the 2nd Battalion 9th Native Infantry, marched from Biana on foot at the head of his battalion and kept it in formation. Of the few European artillery who survived so far, those who reached Fatehpur Sikri were taken prisoners with a Doctor Burgh, and were afterwards barbarously murdered in Holkar's presence for refusing to enter his service.

Monson's report, written at Agra on September 2, does

justice to the courage and loyalty shown by so large a proportion of his force. It concludes with these words:

> I beg leave now to assure your Excellency that the coolness and determined bravery shown by the officers and men of the detachment during this arduous conflict merit my warmest praise; the firmness with which they received the repeated attacks of so superior and powerful an enemy, and the patience with which they underwent the greatest hardships, claim my admiration and gratitude, and showed them worthy of the name of British troops. Your Excellency will perceive by the enclosed return of killed and wounded that our loss has been very great. Though I cannot but lament with the deepest regret the loss of so many noble fellows, yet I cannot but observe with some satisfaction that, even in the hour of death, each emulated the other to deeds of glory, and fell as became British soldiers and men.

The officers selected by Monson for particular mention for the services in the retreat were Lieut.-Colonels Don, M'Culloch, and Ashe; Major Radcliffe; Captains O'Donnell, Nicholl, Fetherston, and Fletcher.

The immediate results of Colonel Monson's disaster were serious. All hopes of a speedy termination of the war vanished, and for a time the safety of Upper India was gravely imperilled. The energy of Lord Wellesley and his Commander-in-Chief, and the brave defence of Delhi, which will presently be described, saved the situation; but permanent injury to British prestige was the result of so serious and complete a reverse. The natives of India had discovered that British armies were not invincible, and the course of this narrative will show the consequence of their discovery. The story of Monson's advance and retreat proves him to have been rash and undecided—hard words to apply to a brave and unfortunate soldier; yet none others will fairly describe his conduct. His recklessness regarding supplies and communications, which had such fatal consequences, cannot be palliated.

Many severe criticisms have been directed against General Lake, both for his selection of Monson for an independent command and for his despatch of the detachment southward from Jaipur at so unfavourable a time of year. As regards the choice of Monson, it does not appear that General Lake can fairly be blamed. He acted with scrupulous fairness at the commencement of the war, dividing the commands of divisions and brigades impartially between the officers of the king's and the Company's armies; and the narrative has shown that in the matter of independent commands he had acted in like manner throughout the operations. Of senior officers who took the field in 1803, General Ware and Colonel Vandeleur had been killed, and General St John had left the army. Of the colonels who had shown themselves fit for command, White was at Gwalior, Blair at Agra, Ochterlony at Delhi, Burn at Saharunpur, Don, in bad health, at Rampura.

Monson, when chosen to command his detachment, was the senior brigadier with the army, and a man who had frequently distinguished himself in action. He had just shown his zeal and military spirit by returning to duty in the field as soon as he had recovered from a dangerous wound. It has been charged against Monson that he was out of sympathy with native troops and had no confidence in them. This may possibly be true, but he had, at least, much longer experience of the Indian Army than had Lake himself, who not only liked his native troops, but was both loved and trusted by them. Monson's defects of character were as yet unknown, and Lake had had no opportunity of detecting them. It seems a fair conclusion that Lake was in no way to blame for his choice of Monson.

As for the unfortunate southward march which caused the disaster, it was not ordered by Lake. He, as far as the writer can ascertain, gave Monson a free hand, merely charging him with the protection of the Rajput states and of the British frontier. It would certainly have been better, as the event showed, had Lake given Monson more definite orders as to the limits of his movements; but to treat a subordinate with generous confidence was natural to Lake, and was a venial sin. A man must have the defects of his qualities, and so it was with Lake.

The defeat of Monson fell as a grievous blow on Lord Wellesley and on Lake, and both accepted it with admirable spirit. The Commander-in-Chief's first thought was to take all the blame on his own shoulders, to suggest excuses both for Monson and Murray, and to attempt to cheer the Governor-General by assurances that the situation should speedily be restored.

Lord Wellesley's response was equally generous. Regarding Monson, whom at the time he believed to be dead, he writes:

> Whatever may have been his fate, or whatever the results of his misfortunes to my own fame, I will endeavour to shield his character from obloquy, nor will I attempt the mean purpose of sacrificing his reputation to save mine. His former services and his zeal entitle him to indulgence. We must endeavour rather to retrieve than to blame what is past.

The letter concludes with expressions of undiminished confidence in Lake, who acted with his usual promptitude and energy. Not a day was lost, for Lake marched from Cawnpore on September 3 at the head of his British troops.

The 8th, 27th. and 29th Light Dragoons, and what was left of the 76th, were still with him. The only newcomers were the newly-raised experimental battery of horse artillery and the flank companies of the 22nd Regiment— a regiment which had an interesting history. It had returned in 1795 to England from the West Indies a mere skeleton, most of the men having died of yellow fever, and the survivors having been drafted to regiments remaining abroad. Recruiting difficulties were great, and every device was being tried to fill the ranks of the army. Three regiments, of which the 22nd was one, were selected as "experimental regiments" in which boys from sixteen to nineteen years old were to be enlisted. Those taken were principally boys who were maintained by their parishes. They came forward in large numbers, and grew into excellent soldiers.

The 22nd served two and a half years in the south of England, went to Guernsey in 1798, and in February 1800 was sent to South Africa. Owing to the disgraceful transport arrangements of the period, over seventy men of the regiment died during the voyage, but the remainder, broken to an iron discipline by the severe methods of the day, hardened into an exceptionally fine regiment. The 22nd moved on to India in February 1803, and the flank companies saw some service in the early portion of the Maratha War with the force under Colonel Harcourt in Cuttack. In January 1804 these companies were ordered from Calcutta to join General Lake's army. John Shipp, a workhouse boy, who had enlisted in 1795 and was now a sergeant in the Light company, states in his memoirs that the flank companies marched from Calcutta to the Biana Pass at the rate of twenty-five or twenty-six miles a-day, and thought nothing of it. The whole army was ordered to assemble at Agra; and although the rains still continued to fall in torrents, and the whole country was inundated, the British corps reached the left bank of the Jumna on September 22. The regiments crossed the river independently, and proceeded to a camp between Agra and Sikandra, commanded by Colonel Macan. Here the army was formed, and was finally allotted to brigades on September 27.

Colonel Macan was placed in command of two brigades of cavalry—the first, under Lieut.-Colonel Vandeleur, consisting of the 8th Light Dragoons and the 2nd, 3rd, and 6th Bengal Cavalry; and the second, commanded by Lieut.-Colonel Brown, comprising the 27th and 29th Light Dragoons and the 1st and 4th Bengal Cavalry.

The infantry, commanded by Major-General Fraser, who had taken the place of Major-General St John, was divided into three brigades. Of these, Brigadier-General Monson again commanded the first, and had under him the 76th, the 1st Battalion 2nd and the 1st Battalion 4th Native Infantry; Brigadier-General G. S. Browne commanded the second brigade (1st and 2nd Battalions 15th and 1st Battalion 21st Native Infantry); and Brigadier-General Ball, the third brigade, of two battalions only— the 1st Battalion 8th and the 2nd Battalion 22nd Native Infantry. In order that Monson's detachment should not feel themselves in disgrace, General Lake took the three most effective battalions, the 1st and 2nd Battalions 12th and the 2nd Battalion 21st, and formed them into a reserve brigade, the command of which was given to Lieut.-Colonel Don. The flank companies of the 22nd Regiment were attached to this brigade.

Lake desired to march against Holkar without delay, and by dint of great exertions was actually able to leave Agra on October 1.

Holkar's horse, though it had shown no great spirit in the pursuit of Monson's detachment, had been bold in the absence of organised resistance. During Lake's march from Cawnpore to Agra it had pushed into British territory and overrun a portion of the Doab, burning, robbing, and murdering as it went. As Holkar approached Muttra on September 15, Colonel Browne, the commandant, who was at the head of a considerable garrison, retired hurriedly on Agra. This was pardonable, for Holkar's strength at this time, according to James Skinner, was 60,000 horse of sorts, 15,000 infantry, and 192 guns. The town of Muttra, with much baggage and a store of grain, fell into the hands of Holkar; great alarm filled the minds of the inhabitants of the Doab; the Jat Raja of Bhartpur, who had become an ally of the British at the time of Laswari, evidently inclined to the cause of the Marathas; and the general aspect of affairs was highly alarming. Lake's arrival at Agra, however, restored confidence, and his decision to employ part of Monson's detachment assured the sepoys that he still confided in their loyalty and fighting quality.

Lake marched from Sikandra, as has been stated, on October 1, and arrived almost unopposed at Muttra three days later. On the first day's march no enemy was seen, but after it the Maratha horse hung about the columns of march and gave Lake hopes of bringing on a general action. Holkar, however, was playing a deep game, for while thus occupying Lake's attention with his cavalry, he despatched his infantry and artillery under his adopted son, Harnat Singh, to attempt the capture of Delhi and the emperor.

This was a brilliant move, and would have succeeded but for the sagacity of Ochterlony, the Resident, who had anticipated some such an attempt, and had prepared to meet it. During the hot weather Delhi had lain without a garrison, except for the regular battalion which formed an escort for the emperor and furnished the Resident's guard.

Lieut.-Colonel Burn, who had originally commanded the troops appointed to watch the city, had been sent with his regiment to Saharunpur, in order to guard against any movement on the part of the Sikhs.

One of Sindhia's battalions, which had been taken into the British service, had similarly been stationed under Major Harriott, its commanding officer, at Rohtak, and another battalion of the same origin, under Lieutenant Birch, was at Panipat. All these outlying detachments were called in by Ochterlony as soon as he heard of the approach of Holkar, but so rapid was the approach of the Marathas that any sluggishness of movement would have been fatal.

Realising the situation, Lieut.-Colonel Burn made forced marches from Saharunpur, covering nearly thirty miles a day, and arrived at Delhi on September 5. The country people rose, for the star of Britain seemed to be declining. Most of Burn's baggage was captured, but he, an experienced soldier, saw that no time was to be lost, and hurried on, allowing the marauders to escape unpunished.

On arriving at Delhi, Burn assumed the command of all the troops there, and prepared to defend the city and palace. The total force, after the concentration, consisted of two battalions and four companies of sepoys; the two irregular battalions from Rohtak and Panipat, each about 400 strong; 400 other irregular matchlock men and a party of irregular horse, about 1200 strong, under Lieutenant Hunter. This seemed to Colonel Burn a very inadequate force with which to defend the seven miles of ruinous walls which surrounded the city of Delhi, particularly as eight companies, or a third of the regular sepoys, were unavailable, being required to garrison the palace and Fort Selimgarh, in which there were reserve provisions for twenty days.

Burn therefore took up a position outside Delhi, and for

more than a month successfully held at a distance the weak parties of Marathas who approached the city. On October 7, however, Ochterlony decided that it was no longer safe for the small force to remain in the open. Burn's irregulars had on several occasions given trouble, and severe measures had been necessary in the case of one corps. On this day, too, the irregular horse had behaved badly, and Ochterlony therefore used his authority as Resident and insisted on Burn retiring into the city. As the infantry marched into Delhi Hunter's horse deserted, the greater part of them going over to the enemy.

Having received definite orders, Burn loyally took up the defence of the city of Delhi, and found before him the following task: with 1400 regular sepoys, 1100 irregulars, and 11 guns, to defend seven miles of ruinous walls pierced by many gates against a force of 10,000 infantry, 8000 cavalry, with 160 guns. The enemy could choose his point of attack, and was defended by the immense army of Holkar himself against anything that General Lake might attempt in aid of the besieged.

The task committed to Burn would have been a hopeless one but for the wise forethought exercised by Ochterlony during Burn's month of active operations outside Delhi. In this period Ochterlony had to some extent repaired the walls, and had constructed redoubts for the defence of the principal gates. Burn, on entering the city, allotted small garrisons to these redoubts, and posted the remainder of his force in selected positions along the walls. So inadequate was the number of men available to the space to be guarded that no relief could be furnished. Every man, therefore, had to cook his food on his post and there get what rest he could.

The atrocities committed by Holkar on the prisoners and wounded of Monson's force now recoiled on his head. The defenders of Delhi determined to hold their post to the last, and never by surrender to risk having to endure similar cruelties.

Burn's troops were hardly distributed in their positions when, early in the morning of October 8, the Maratha army, under Harnat Singh, were seen advancing through the ravines and filing off in every direction so as to envelop the city of Delhi. Operations quickly began, for at nine o'clock the Marathas brought several large guns into action and opened a heavy fire on the north-east bastion, on which an 18-pounder was mounted. The defences of this gun were soon destroyed, and it was found necessary to withdraw it lest its own fire should bring down the bastion.

As it appeared that this was likely to be the point of assault, a battery for three guns was constructed on a height behind the bastion, and the defences were otherwise strengthened. In the course of the night the Marathas constructed a very fine battery mounting twenty-four guns, and dug trenches for two battalions to guard it; and although the distance from the wall was too great, they had, by the evening of October 10, made three practicable breaches, in spite of the unremitting exertions of the garrison to repair the damage. A heavy fire was also kept up on other portions of the wall, but it seemed evident that an assault on the three breaches near the north-east bastion was intended. Colonel Burn therefore decided that a sortie was necessary, which was made the same night (October 10) by a party of 300 picked men. This party was led by Lieutenant John Rose, an officer of nine years' service, who had been severely wounded and had highly distinguished himself at the capture of Agra.

Lieutenant Rose's party carried out their duty on this occasion with complete success, reaching the battery unobserved. Charging into the trenches, they drove away the gunners and infantry in the vicinity, spiked the guns, and returned, having suffered very slight loss. This spirited sortie so alarmed the Marathas that they abandoned the low ground altogether, and the garrison was able to repair the breaches unmolested.

On the morning of October 11 the enemy turned their attention to the wall near the Delhi gate, and also at a place near the Turkoman gate, making considerable breaches at both places. The first breach was repaired during the night, and no further attempt was made at that point; but as the ruins near the Turkoman gate afforded much cover and served as ready-made batteries and trenches, the wall in that region was severely battered, and the breach there soon became practicable. This danger was met by Burn by the construction of an inner line of defence, consisting of strongly constructed parapets.

The Marathas, while keeping up a heavy fire on the breach, assailed these new works by mining, and, had more time been available, would doubtless thus have taken Delhi. On October 13 they discovered that General Lake was approaching with his army, and having no wish to be caught between two fires, they resolved to attempt an immediate assault. Accordingly, on the morning of October 14, the Maratha artillery opened a very heavy fire on selected points in all portions of the wall of Delhi save on the side washed by the Jumna, and soon after sunrise their infantry was seen advancing in large bodies with scaling-ladders against the points selected for escalade. The attempts, however, were made with little vigour, and were all repulsed. The Marathas retired, leaving their ladders on the ground. There was some expectation of a second attempt at night, but none was made, and in the morning of October 15 it was found that the Marathas had abandoned the siege.

In spite of the want of spirit shown by the enemy, the defence of Delhi by Burn and Ochterlony must be regarded as a fine feat of arms; for it was undertaken at a time when an adverse tide was flowing, and the disparity of men and guns was very great.

The loyalty of the irregular portion of the garrison was also doubtful, and it is on this account that Burn and Ochterlony deserve so much credit for their decision to risk all and to hold the city as well as the fortress. Less determined men would have found fair reason to abandon the larger task, and would have been satisfied to hold the fort and palace alone. Nor must the fine courage and discipline of the sepoys be forgotten, for both were tried to the utmost by the manner in which they were distributed among scattered posts, with full knowledge that a treacherous surrender in any part of the defences would seal the doom of every man wearing the Company's uniform.

Recognising that the character of the defence threw exceptional responsibility on junior officers, General Lake bestowed the honour of a mention in General Orders on a large number of those who had distinguished themselves. Having eulogised the "skill and fortitude" shown by Lieut.-Colonel Burn, and the "wise and timely precautions" taken by Ochterlony, special mention was accorded to Lieutenants Rose, Evans, Heathcote, Dickson, and Locket, the subalterns who led the sortie. Captains Harriott and Carnegie and Lieutenants Woodville and Birch, officers who had abandoned Sindhia's service at the beginning of the war, were also mentioned, as were Lieutenants Lindsay and Hunter, cavalry officers who "handsomely volunteered their services."

Not satisfied with this reward, General Lake consistently devoted his patronage as Commander-in-Chief in furthering the interests of officers who had rendered good service in the field or had been disabled by wounds.

The name of the gallant commandant of Delhi in the

defence of the city in October 1804 is still preserved, for Burn's Bastion is so called in his honour.

The most able criticism of Monson's operations is contained in a private letter written by the Duke of Wellington at Calcutta in September 1804. The Duke, then Sir Arthur Wellesley, wrote with a full knowledge of all the circumstances, and he was well acquainted with Monson. It may be added that in all his long life the Duke never wrote an unfair criticism of an operation of war.

Sir Robert Peel, in speaking of the Duke of Wellington, said that he considered him the most powerful writer in the English language, and that the letter upon Colonel Monson's retreat was the best military letter he had ever read. In addition to this testimony there is on record an interesting letter by General Sir Charles Napier, written shortly after the battle of Miani, in which he says:

> The Duke's letter on the retreat of Colonel Monson decided me never to retire before an Indian army. If I have done wrong abstractedly (for success, like charity, covers sins), the Great Master led me into it: but my own conviction is that I have done right; and that my admiration of him, and study of his words and deeds, as the great rules of war, have caused this victory.

A letter so admired by Peel, and taken by Charles Napier as his guide in a critical moment, is surely worthy of the attention of students of the art of war.

Fort William
September 12, 1804
You will have heard reports of poor Monson's reverses, but as I am on the spot, you will be glad to hear the truth from me; and as they give some important military lessons to us all, I do not regard the trouble of writing them to you. When it became necessary to

attack Holkar, Monson was detached from the grand army with three battalions and their guns, and a body of cavalry under Lieutenant Lucan. Holkar, who was then near Ajmeer with an army composed only of horse (and as Gen. Lake was at no great distance from Monson), retreated towards Malwa.

After quitting the river Jumna and passing through the flat country depending on Agra, the first country going to the southward is a mountainous tract called Jeypoor, governed by the Rajah of that name, who had been tributary to Scindiah and Holkar previous to the late war, and who had been relieved from his tribute by the operation of the treaty of peace. Joining to the territory of Jeypoor is that of the Rajah of Boondy, of the same description; and joining to Boondy is the territory of the Rajah of Kota. These last two Rajahs had been, and are still, tributary to Scindiah; and Holkar has claims upon them which they hoped to get rid of by the British assistance, in consequence of their conduct in the war; at all events they were desirous to obtain for a time British protection against the demands of Holkar.

Between Boondy and Jeypoor is a small territory and fort called Rampoora, which at the commencement of the war belonged to Holkar. This territory had formerly been part of the Jeypoor territory, and had been seized by the Holkar family in some of their former contests with the Rajah of Jeypoor. The whole of this country between Agra and the province of Malwa, which joins to the Kota territory and which is entered through a pass called the Muckundra *ghaut*, is intersected by rivers and *nullahs*, which are either full throughout the western rains or are filled at times by those rains, and become impassable for troops. Of these the principal is the river Chumbul, which runs between Kota and Boondy, and the river Banas, which runs between Rampoora and Agra.

When Holkar fled in front of the army of the Commander-in-Chief, Col. Monson followed him successively to Boondy and Kota, the Rajahs of which countries were very desirous to have the protection of the British troops against his exactions, and promised supplies and everything which Col. Monson could want. At the same time that Col. Monson advanced, a detachment under Col. Don, consisting of two battalions, was sent to take Rampoora, of which place it got possession by storm; and this detachment afterwards joined and reinforced Monson's corps, which then consisted of five battalions.

In the month of June the Commander-in-Chief withdrew his army into cantonments, leaving Monson's corps in the Kota country. Monson, towards the end of that month, passed through the Muckundra *ghaut* into Malwa, accompanied by the troops of the Rajah of Kota, and some of Scindiah's, under Bappojee Scindiah, and attacked and took by storm the hill fort of Hinglisghur; and after this operation he took up a position in Malwa, recommended to him by the Rajah of Kota, at some distance from the Muckundra *ghaut*, in which the Rajah told him he was likely to get supplies, and from which Monson expected to be able to communicate with Col. Murray, at that time on his march from Guzerat towards Ougein.

After his retreat in front of the Commander-in-Chief Holkar had first threatened Ougein, and afterwards gone to Mundissoor, a town belonging to Scindiah, situated to the north-west of Ougein, and on the left of the Chumbul. Between the middle and latter end of June he took and plundered this town; and at that time the river Chumbul was between him and Col. Monson, who was encamped about five *coss* from the river, on the right bank.

Towards the beginning of July Holkar passed the Chumbul with his army. Col. Monson learnt that he was doing so, and intended to attack him. He moved towards the place at which he heard Holkar was, and found that the whole army had crossed the river; nearly about the same time, he understood that Col. Murray, who had made two marches towards Ougein from Guzerat, had recrossed the Myhie; and upon the whole, Monson, having only two days' provisions, thought it best to retreat. Accordingly he sent off his baggage early on the following morning, the 8th July I believe, towards the Muckundra ghaut; and he followed with the infantry at about nine in the morning, meaning to reach Muckundra that night, the distance about seventeen miles. He left Lucan, with his irregular horse and Bappojee Scindiah's horse, to cover his rear, and to follow as his rear-guard.

After Monson had marched a few miles he heard that Holkar had attacked with his cavalry his rear-guard of irregular horse, and shortly afterwards he received intelligence that the rear-guard was destroyed and Lucan taken prisoner. He arrived at Muckundra unmolested and took up a position that covered the *ghaut*, but which, like all others that I have seen, had many passages practicable for cavalry.

On the next day, or the next but one, Monson was attacked by the whole of Holkar's cavalry in three separate bodies, who, however, could make no impression on him, and they were beat off. Towards evening he heard that the infantry was arrived at a camp within two or three *coss* of the Muckundra *ghaut*, with their guns, 175 in number, and he determined to retreat again. He accordingly marched to Kota, the Rajah of which place urged him to stay there, but could not supply him with provisions; and then Monson marched on the following day and crossed the Chumbul in boats provided by the Rajah, which he sunk after he had crossed.

The rain began about the 10th July and became incessant, and rendered Monson's marches much more difficult than they would otherwise have been, particularly in that country, which is a black cotton soil. At last, after he had crossed the Chumbul, he was obliged to spike his guns and leave them behind; and he continued his march, getting but little provision on the road until he reached Rampoora. He was followed, but not much harassed, by a body of Holkar's horse, which overtook him at a *nullah*, which, being full, stopped him. He twice beat up the camp of this body of horse, and then I believe they quitted him. On his arrival at Rampoora, Monson was joined by two battalions with their guns, and a body of Hindustani horse under Major Frith, which had been sent from Agra to reinforce him, and he immediately began to collect provisions at Rampoora.

The rains which had been so distressing to Monson likewise impeded Holkar, some of whose guns remained to the southward of the Muckundra *ghaut*. His progress to the northward was likewise impeded by Monson having destroyed the Rajah of Kota's boats on the Chumbul. However, at last he advanced, and towards the 20th August again approached Monson at Rampoora.

By this time Monson had collected only about twelve days' provisions, and the Commander-in-Chief, foreseeing the difficulty in which he might again be involved, desired him on the 20th August to retire towards Jeypoor, if he should think it probable that he might be distressed for provisions. Monson, however, remained till Holkar approached him within six *coss* with his whole army, and on the 21st August, in the evening, commenced his retreat towards Agra by Kooshalghur, leaving Jeypoor on his left hand.

He left fifteen companies as a garrison in Rampoora. He arrived at Banas river on the 23rd, and found that it was full; on the 24th, in the morning, it fell and became fordable, and he passed over his baggage and a battalion, and between twelve and three o'clock he passed over three more battalions, leaving the picquets and one battalion to support them on the southern bank.

Holkar's troops had appeared in the morning, and were seen crossing at different fords on the right and left flank; and towards evening Holkar's infantry and guns appeared in front. They attacked the picquets, but were repulsed; and the picquets and battalion took eight guns; but afterwards our troops were overpowered by superior numbers and were obliged to retreat across the river to the main body, in which operation they lost many men, being attacked on their rear, and also by the horse who had crossed the river and moved up its bed. Monson retreated from Banas river on the night of the 24th, leaving his baggage, and arrived at Kooshalghur, about forty miles distant, on the night of the 25th.

He was followed throughout the march by Holkar's horse, who, however, were not able to make any impression on him. He halted on the night of the 25th and the 26th at Kooshalghur, and on the 26th at night marched towards Agra. Something happened on the 27th of which I have not received an account, but on the 30th Monson and his detachment arrived at Agra. The Commander-in-Chief has taken the field, and it is to be hoped that he will have an early opportunity of wiping away the disgrace which we have suffered.

It is worthwhile to review these transactions, in order that we may see to what these misfortunes ought to be attributed, that in future, if possible, they may be avoided.

In the first place, it appears that Col. Monson's corps was never so strong as to be able to engage Holkar's army, if that chief should collect it; at least the Colonel was of that opinion. Secondly, it appears that it had not any stock of provisions. Thirdly, that it depended for provisions upon certain Rajahs who urged its advance. Fourthly, that no measures whatever were taken by British officers to collect provisions either at Boondy or Kota, or even at Rampoora, a fort belonging to us, in which we had a British garrison. Fifthly, that the detachment was advanced to such a distance, over so many almost impassable rivers and *nullahs*, without any boats collected or posts upon those rivers; and in fact, that the detachment owes its safety to the Rajah of Kota, who supplied them with his boats.

The result of these facts is an opinion in my mind that the detachment must have been lost, even if Holkar had not attacked them with his infantry and cavalry.

In respect to the conduct of the operations, it is my opinion that Monson ought to have attacked Holkar in the first instance. If he chose to retire, he ought have supported the rear-guard with his infantry, and to have sent the irregular horse away with the baggage.

When he began to retreat, he ought not to have stopped longer than a night at Muckundra; because he must have been certain that the same circumstances which obliged him to retire to Muckundra would also oblige him to quit that position. The difference between a good and a bad military position is nothing when the troops are starving.

The same reasoning holds good respecting Monson's halt at Rampoora, unless he intended to fight. As he had been reinforced, he ought to have fallen back till he was certain of his supplies; and having waited till Holkar approached him, and particularly as Holkar's army was not then in great strength in infantry and guns, he ought to have vigorously attacked him before he retired. When his picquets were attacked on the Banas, he ought to have supported them with his whole corps, leaving one battalion on the northern bank to take care of his baggage; and if he had done so, he probably would have gained a victory, would have saved his baggage, and regained his honour.

We have some important lessons from this campaign. First, we should never employ a corps on a service for which it is not fully equal. Secondly, against the Mahrattas in particular, but against all enemies, we should take care to be sure of plenty of provisions. Thirdly, experience has shown us that British troops can never depend upon Rajahs, or any allies, for their supplies. Our own officers must purchase them; and if we should employ a native in such an important service, we ought to see the supplies before we venture to expose our troops in the situation in which they may want them. Fourthly, when we have a fort which can support our operations, such as Rampoora to the northward, or Ahmednugger, or Chandore, in your quarter, we should immediately adopt effectual measures to fill it with provisions and stores in case of need. Fifthly, when we cross a river likely to be full in the rains, we ought to have a post and boats upon it—as I have upon all the rivers south of Poonah, and as you have, I hope, upon the Beemah and the Godavery.

In respect to the operations of a corps in the situation of Monson's, they must be decided and quick; and in all retreats it must be recollected that they are safe and easy in proportion to the number of attacks made by the retreating corps. But attention to the foregoing observations will, I hope, prevent a British corps from retreating.

Sir Arthur Wellesley lived to witness the destruction, in 1842, of a British army through the neglect of the principles so clearly laid down by him in the above letter; and if the Great Master's advice was ignored in his lifetime, it may be of use to reproduce it a century after it was written. The conditions of war may change, but its principles remain the same.

CHAPTER 4

The Siege of Bhartpur

While Holkar's infantry and artillery were endeavouring to capture Delhi, their master was doing his best to avoid contact with General Lake's small army. Holkar was well aware that an encounter with Lake, with his dreaded European troops, would not be willingly risked by his army; nor in spite of his boast to General Wellesley, written in the previous February, "General Lake shall not have leisure to breathe for a moment," did he show any desire to measure his skill against that of the Commander-in-Chief. It seemed easier to him, and more in accordance with the character of his army, to carry out the remainder of his threat, "countries of many hundred *kos* shall be overrun and plundered, and calamities will fall on *lakhs* of human beings in continual war, by the attacks of my army, which overwhelms like the waves of the sea."

It was related in the last chapter that Muttra fell into the hands of Holkar on September 15, and was reoccupied by General Lake on October 3. On the following day a convoy of 100 camels, bringing grain to the army from Agra, was captured, with its escort of convalescent sepoys. This happened at the village of Aring, under the very nose of Lake's army, and, according to Skinner's memoirs, several other convoys of grain were captured about the same time, owing to the great numerical strength of the enemy.

There was, in consequence, something approaching starvation in Lake's camp, six pounds of coarse flour, the common food of the sepoys, selling for a rupee. Lake made two attempts to bring Holkar's horse to action, marching from his camp on October 7 and 10 at such an hour as to arrive at the Maratha outposts a few minutes before dawn. On these occasions the infantry made a direct approach, while the cavalry made an enveloping movement; but the Marathas were nervously on the alert, and were found in the saddle, warning having been given by rockets and signal-fires.

On October 7 a few Marathas only were killed by the galloper guns, while on the 10th, though the British cavalry swept at a gallop through the Maratha camp, Holkar's horsemen scattered in every direction and suffered but little loss. When, however, after these affairs, the British turned to retrace their footsteps to Muttra, the Marathas, writes Thorn, who was present, "dashed on, attacking our rear and flanks, firing long shots with their matchlocks, while those who were armed with spears and *tulwars* (swords) flourished their weapons, making at the same time a noise like jackals by way of bravado." On the second occasion about thirty Marathas were killed and several captured, who expected to be put to death in retaliation for the atrocities committed upon Monson's men. General Lake, however, gave each prisoner a rupee and put them at liberty, sending a message to Holkar "that none but cowards treated their prisoners with cruelty."

Lake now received information of the siege of Delhi from Colonel Ochterlony, and was anxious to march to the relief of the hard-pressed garrison. This, however, was impossible without supplies, which depended on the arrival of a Brinjari convoy from Cawnpore. There had been a great scarcity of food for six days, the native troops were uneasy in mind, and Skinner states that Lake found it necessary to post a sepoy with each trooper vidette, with orders to shoot the trooper should he attempt to desert.

Skinner was asked by General Lake to attempt to bring the Brinjari convoy into camp, and with this object made a most gallant night march of thirty-five miles at the head of 1200 of his horse. By good management and determination Skinner succeeded in bringing in the whole convoy of 60,000 bullocks laden with flour, which provided seven days' rations for the army. This was a priceless service, which Lake recognised by presenting Skinner with his own sword and 20,000 rupees (£2000).

Lake was now able to start for Delhi, and set out on October 12. His cavalry led the way, followed by the baggage and bazaars, which marched along the bank of the Jumna, the infantry in column guarding the exposed flank. Holkar could do nothing to retard the march of the army while in this secure formation, though he made feeble attacks on October 13 and 17, which were repulsed at the cost of a few casualties.

On October 18 Delhi was reached; but the Maratha besieging force had gone away four days earlier, and were now followed by their main body, which retired about four days' march from Delhi in a northerly direction. General Lake desired to pursue Holkar at once, and issued immediate orders for the army to deposit half its camp equipage at Delhi and to march on October 19.

Sufficient supplies, however, were not obtainable, and it was represented to Lake that it would be useless to pursue Holkar with weary transport animals, his guns being drawn by the best bullocks in India, assisted by an ample supply of elephants.

A halt at Delhi was therefore imperative; but on October 26 Lieut.-Colonel Burn was despatched to his former post, Saharunpur, where it was thought desirable to re-establish a garrison in order to keep an eye on the southern Sikhs. Three days later Holkar suddenly took the offensive, crossed the Jumna near Panipat, and overtook Burn on his march near Shamli, a town about sixty-four miles north-east of Delhi.

Burn's detachment consisted of his own battalion, the 2nd Battalion 14th Native Infantry, and an irregular battalion, with six guns. He was attacked almost immediately after crossing the Jumna; but being a resolute man, and knowing that Mr Guthrie, the magistrate at Saharunpur, was besieged by the Sikhs, he determined to push on by forced marches, and, if possible, thus keep ahead of the Marathas.

Unfortunately, Burn was delayed on the road on October 28 by the breakdown of one of his gun-carriages, and on the following day, outside Shamli, the Marathas appeared in great strength, commanded by Holkar himself. Burn was anxious that Holkar should attack him; but the Marathas showed no such intention, contenting themselves, as stated in Burn's narrative, with "sniping" his men from the shelter of the surrounding jungle.

Early on October 30, Burn, finding that he could not advance through the jungle owing to the great number of the Marathas, and feeling confident that Lake would soon hear of his situation and come to his relief, took refuge in a walled enclosure furnished with small bastions at the four corners. Believing that Burn would be unable to mount his guns, the Marathas came in close to the walls. After great labour, however, four 6-pounders were got up on the bastions, which opened unexpectedly on the enemy with great effect. The Marathas constantly threatened the detachment with assault, and exhibited ladders, thereby keeping them on the alert. They also erected platforms from which they were able to fire into the crowded troops, causing heavy loss. Among other casualties, an officer who was pointing one of the guns was shot from one of these platforms, losing the sight of both his eyes.

The Marathas confidently expected to compel the detachment to surrender, for the troops had been unable to take any grain with them into the fort, and the only food at first obtainable was the sheep and goats taken by the officers for their own supply. These were carefully distributed among those who would eat meat, but many of the sepoys were Hindus of high caste, who, as a matter of course, refused it, and were consequently reduced to starvation. Lieutenant Rose, the officer who led the sortie from Delhi, performed a similar service at Shamli, and headed a foraging party, which brought in some scanty supplies.

In spite of their very severe sufferings and losses, Colonel Burn's detachment showed a noble fortitude and loyalty, refusing all the bribes offered them by Holkar if they would betray their officers. On November 3 General Lake relieved Shamli, arriving from Delhi, after a forced march of four days, with six regiments of cavalry and the reserve brigade of infantry under Lieut.-Colonel Don. These marches formed the first stage of Lake's pursuit of Holkar, one of the most remarkable marches on record. Colonel Burn's detachment was reduced to a very weak state from starvation, and nearly a hundred sepoys had been killed.

The townsmen of Shamli had combined with the Marathas against Colonel Burn's detachment, and General Lake consequently gave up the town to plunder as an example to others.

Mr Guthrie, hearing that Burn was besieged at Shamli, had provided for his own safety by placing himself under the protection of the Begum Sumru. Lake therefore decided that it was unnecessary to garrison Saharunpur at this stage, and, for the time being, carried Colonel Burn's detachment to Meerut, where he left it to watch the course of events.

We must now revert to General Lake's march in pursuit of Holkar, and, to make matters clear, must return for a moment to Delhi. It will be remembered that when Burn's detachment left that city, Lake was engaged in collecting supplies and transport, in order to bring Holkar to action. Information was presently obtained that the Maratha infantry and guns had retired towards Dig—or Deeg, to use the spelling then in vogue—while Holkar himself, with the bulk of his cavalry, had moved in the direction of Shamli.

General Lake, therefore, set out with a small force, as has been stated, on October 31, in pursuit of Holkar, while he despatched the remainder of his army, under Major-General Fraser, to deal with the infantry and artillery before Dig.

There was at first no reason to suppose that Holkar would have caught up Burn's detachment, that event having only been brought about by the unfortunate mischance to his gun, and Lake's two first marches were consequently of reasonable length, as is advisable after a halt. The first march, to Loni, was ten miles, and the second, to Bhagpat, fourteen miles. Lake then heard of Burn's position, and, on November 2, marched from Bhagpat to Kandla, twenty-seven miles. Early on the following day he marched the eleven remaining miles to Shamli, and effected the relief. On November 4 the force halted.

Not to weary the reader by a string of marches with unpronounceable names, it may suffice to say that from November 5 to 17 Lake's force marched continuously until on the latter date they found their quarry, and, what is yet more remarkable, Don's reserve brigade of infantry kept with them, march by march, until on the last day the distance and pace went beyond the powers of even that admirable brigade. From October 31 to November 17 the total distance covered in this march by the infantry and baggage was 325 miles by the map—an average of 18 miles a-day, including the halt day.

The actual distance covered by the cavalry and horse artillery was considerably greater, and was estimated by Captain Thorn, who was Brigade-Major of Cavalry to Colonel Macan, at 25 miles a-day, during the last fourteen marches.

It is worth remembering, as bearing on the working powers of young Indian soldiers, that one of the infantry battalions which performed this feat of marching was the 2nd Battalion 21st Native Infantry, not a man of which had been over twenty-two years old when the battalion joined the army. The 21st and 12th, the latter a veteran corps, had also recently maintained their efficiency under the hardships of Monson's retreat.

Throughout Lake's pursuit of Holkar through the Doab, the Marathas always kept from twenty-five to thirty miles ahead, burning and destroying as they went along. When, however, Aliganj was reached, on October 16, the village was found still burning, and Holkar was reported to be near Farakhabad (the native city near Fatehgarh), twenty-six miles ahead.

The distance covered that day had been twenty-three miles, but General Lake decided to make a night march to surprise the enemy, and so save the garrison of Fatehgarh. Accordingly, at nine o'clock in the evening, he moved on again with the three British cavalry regiments and Captain Clement Brown's battery of Horse Artillery, without any baggage whatever, leaving the remainder of the force to follow on next day. Just as the Light Dragoons were mounting, the good news reached General Lake that General Fraser had defeated Holkar's infantry brigades at Dig, and this intelligence made the cavalry doubly anxious to come up with the boasted Maratha horse, in order to give the finishing stroke to Holkar's power. Thorn, in his interesting account of the march, adds that the moon was up, and the night mild and pleasant, so that everyone was cheered by the hope of finishing, by the night's work, their late harassing marches. The intelligence department was admirably conducted by Major Salkeld, and reports concerning the enemy were received by him at intervals during the march.

Just at daybreak on October 17, the head of the British column reached the outskirts of the enemy's camp. They found the horses still picketed, while the Marathas, wrapped in their blankets, slept beside them. There were no outposts, and the first warning of the approach of Lake was given by the discharge of several rounds of grape from the Horse Artillery, directed where the enemy lay most thickly.

The 8th Light Dragoons, who were leading, galloped into the camp, charging and cutting down the Marathas in every direction, the 27th and 29th doing the same as soon as they could come up; so that in a short time the whole plain was covered with dead bodies. The Marathas had no thought but flight, and Holkar was among the first to escape. He, like Lake, had heard of the battle of Dig on the previous evening, and the bad news had kept him awake all night, though he had not informed his officers of what had happened. His spies had told him of Lake's position at Aliganj, thirty miles away, and we may fairly imagine Holkar calculating on having time to destroy the small garrison of Fatehgarh next morning, and to capture (or slay, according to his fancy) the European civil servants and merchants.

Shortly before the British cavalry arrived at the Maratha camp, an ammunition wagon belonging to Captain Brown's battery blew up. Holkar heard and was alarmed by the sound, but his servants assured him that it was the usual morning gun at Fatehgarh. Soon afterwards came the roar of Brown's guns at close quarters, followed by the trampling of many horses and the wild shouts of the Royal Irish Light Dragoons. Holkar was in the saddle in a moment, and fled, protected by his faithful bodyguard, not stopping, it is said, till he was eighteen miles on the way to Mainpuri. The Marathas were hunted in every direction for ten miles, and most authorities agree that not less than 3000 of them fell in the charge and pursuit. Thorn, who was present, says that many, whose horses were more exhausted than those of the British cavalry, climbed for safety into the mango-trees that grew thickly around. Here they might have escaped but for their rash courage in opening fire with their matchlocks on the rear squadrons of the dragoons as they came up. They were therefore discovered and pistolled, so that numbers tumbled lifeless from the trees. Thorn calculated that, by the time they had ridden back into camp at Farakhabad, the British cavalry had covered considerably over seventy miles in twenty-four hours—an effort, as he remarks, "probably unparalleled in the annals of military history, especially when it is remembered that it was made after a long and harassing march of 350 miles in the space of a fortnight."

Thorn gives his distances in round numbers, but he is a careful writer, narrating facts within his own knowledge; and as cavalry always covers much more ground than is estimated by following marches on the map, his calculation may be taken as an accurate description of a remarkable exploit.

Lake's loss in this affair was very slight, only two dragoons being killed and about twenty wounded. There were also seventy-five casualties among the horses. Holkar's loss was far from being limited to the number killed at Farakhabad. It is, indeed, stated by several writers that half his force deserted after the surprise, and returned to their homes. This defection is said to have amounted to 30,000 men. Holkar's intention in making for Farakhabad had been to plunder the town, which was rich and prosperous, carrying on a considerable trade with other places on the Ganges. He had already (on October 16) burned part of the barracks and officers' bungalows at Fatehgarh, as the cantonment was called, and nothing could have saved the European civilian population and garrison but the wonderful march of Lake and his Light Dragoons.

The British force halted two days at Fatehgarh to rest after their exertions, during which time the Horse Artillery battery had the pleasure of firing three royal salutes for as many victories—their own, that of General Fraser at Dig, and for the capture of Chandur, Holkar's only stronghold in the Deccan, which had been taken by a force under Colonel Wallace.

On the morning of October 19 the reserve brigade and other troops arrived at Fatehgarh from Aliganj: among them was Skinner's Horse; and in the evening General Lake ordered Skinner to pursue Holkar and find out where he had gone. Skinner accordingly left all his baggage, sick men, and galled horses, and started off with 600 sowars at 2 a.m. on October 20. He reached Mainpuri that same evening in time to save the lives of the officers and civilians there, Holkar having heard that Lake was coming up, and having hurriedly fled again. On the 21st Skinner again came up with Holkar and took a hundred prisoners. On these men Skinner played a trick which he relates with great glee in his memoirs.

> Telling them that my corps considered them as brethren, I gave them their liberty, but advised them to take care not to fall into the hands of the dragoons, who were but a few hours behind, and bade them give my salaam to Holkar.

148

Thankful for this treatment, Holkar's sowars improved on their instructions, telling him that they had seen General Lake and his dragoons.

This made him fly faster than ever, but I kept hanging on his rear, marching 20 to 25 *kos* a day (40 to 50 miles) until he crossed the Jumna near Muttra. In this hard seven days' work I had no provisions but what the fields afforded, and neither tents nor bazaar with us. The horses were never unsaddled, and we rested with the *bagdoor* (halter) in our hands all night, having frequently to change our ground two or three times during each night to avoid a surprise from Holkar. In this pursuit I acquired great plunder in horses and camels. We lived on the green *jowar* that was standing in the fields, which we prepared by husking it out and putting it into large pots, adding *ghee* and meat, and boiling the whole together. It was then served out in earthen pots, my share being always brought me by the men, who showed me great love and attention, and were willing to act as my private servants, and tried in every way to please me and add to my comfort; but I felt the want of my dram.

Four days after . . . General Lake arrived, and the corps paraded to receive him. He came up and praised them highly, promised that their services should never be forgotten, and said that they had, by their exertions, secured permanent bread for their lives. On me also he bestowed high commendations, giving me a horse with silver trappings, which had been sent him by some Rajah, and told me to go back to Alleegurh and rest for a month, and recruit my corps to 1700 strong, for he should soon require my services again.

This interesting passage affords a vivid picture of the old

irregular Indian cavalry at their work, and shows also how well Lake knew how to secure their devotion.

On October 20 General Lake's force marched from Fatehgarh for Dig, towards which fortress Holkar and the remainder of his force were reported to have retired. As Lake went on his way he found more and more proof of the terrible losses suffered by the Marathas at Farakhabad. The villages were all full of wounded, most of whom died.

The Zemindars and people of the Doab, who before that action had all been ready to join Holkar and turn against the British, were now full of protestations of loyalty. They had only been deterred from, showing their hand by the punishment of the town of Shamli, and that well-timed act of severity had doubtless averted infinitely greater and more widespread suffering—a lesson that English sentimentalists would do well to remember.

In letters to Lord Mornington, written immediately after his arrival at Fatehgarh, Lake congratulated himself on the complete success of his march. Had it failed in any way, he stated, the Sikhs and Rohillas would all have joined Holkar, and the whole of Upper India would have been in arms against the British. As it was, the Bhartpur Raja, who owed everything to them, had alone thrown off all disguise. For this hostility Lake declared that the Raja must be immediately punished—a suggestion which was formally approved by Lord Mornington. The Raja, indeed, deserves no sympathy. The ruler of the very ancient tribe of Jats, Raja Ranjit Singh of Bhartpur, became a tributary of Madhaji Sindhia in 1785. He was among the first to desert his master and form an alliance with the British after Lake's victory before Delhi. He now, thinking from Monson's reverse that the tide had turned, again changed his side. Raja Ranjit Singh, who must not be confused with his famous namesake and contemporary the ruler of the Sikhs, possessed a fortress of great size and strength in Bhartpur, the capital town of his state, which is said at this time to have contained 50,000 fighting men within its massive ramparts of beaten mud.

Before dealing with General Lake's unfortunate operations against this formidable fortress we must, however, return to Delhi and follow the operations of the force left there, under Major-General Fraser, when Lake set out on his hunt after Holkar.

General Fraser, whose force on leaving Delhi consisted of the 76th Regiment and six battalions of Native Infantry, with about twenty 6-pounder guns, marched from the Moghul capital on November 5, and on reaching Govardhan, about eight miles from Dig, on November 10, was joined by the 1st Bengal European Regiment. His total strength was still under 6000 men.

Dig, or Deeg, as the name used to be written, is a fortified town standing on a rocky site twenty miles east of Muttra, and is a part of the State of Bhartpur. On November 11 General Fraser reconnoitred the Maratha position, and moved at night to a position about two and a half miles east of Dig, close to the village of Bheij. Between this village and Dig was a marsh.

The Maratha army, consisting of twenty-four battalions, a considerable number of horse, and 160 guns, more than half of which were 16 or 18-pounders, was encamped between the fortress of Dig and the village of Kasba Au. This village, which was fortified, guarded the Maratha right, and their left rested on Dig, the garrison of which place now openly showed the alliance of their Raja with Holkar.

On November 12 Major-General Fraser continued his observation of the Maratha position, and in spite of the great strength of the enemy and their advantageous position, decided to attack. The small British force marched at three o'clock in the morning of November 13, two battalions of Native Infantry forming the 3rd Brigade, with the irregular horse, being detailed as escort to the baggage, with orders to follow the advance. The whole attacking force marched round the intervening swamp and made towards the Maratha right. On approaching the village of Kasba Au the advance of the British column was observed and the Marathas opened a distant fire. General Fraser now deployed his force into two lines, each brigade forming one line and the European battalions taking the centre of each line. The cavalry was placed on the left, that flank being threatened by the enemy's horse.

As soon as the infantry had deployed, the village of Kasba Au was carried without difficulty. This village, as is commonly the case in India, stood on a slight eminence, and from it the enemy's position could be clearly seen, consisting of a succession of batteries and entrenchments running back almost to the walls of Dig.

As the 1st Brigade issued from the village they came under a severe cross-fire of artillery; but the 76th instantly ran forward down the hill and captured the nearest battery, bayoneting the Maratha gunners at their post.

The charge of the 76th had carried them far in advance of the remaining battalions of the 1st Brigade, and when the 2nd Brigade cleared the village, their centre battalion, the Bengal European Regiment, rushed forward to the support of the 76th. The Native Infantry battalions on the left of each line advanced to the support of the British battalions, but those on the right (the 1st Battalion 2nd, and the 2nd Battalion 15th) took ground to the right, under Major Hammond, to check a threatened attack by a large body of Marathas from the lower end of the swamp. General Fraser accompanied the Bengal Europeans, and was mortally wounded in the captured battery, his leg being carried off by a cannon-shot. The command consequently devolved on Brigadier-General Monson.

Monson, quite in his element, cheered on the infantry, who captured battery after battery at the point of the bayonet, until they came under the close fire of Dig and suffered considerable loss. In the meantime, a body of the enemy's horse came round, re-took the guns in the position first captured by the 76th, and turned them against our troops. The reserve brigade had not yet come up, and there was no one to stop this dangerous fire until Captain Norford of the 76th, with only twenty-eight men, charged back and again captured the guns, losing his own life in performing this gallant and valuable exploit.

During all this time the two Native Infantry battalions which had moved off to guard the right flank had been hard pressed by the superior artillery-fire of the enemy. Brigadier-General Monson, however, finding it necessary to draw back from the fortress of Dig, and seeing the situation of Major Hammond's two battalions, now brought the fire of several of his guns to bear on the brigade of Marathas opposed to Hammond. Under the fire of his guns Monson also brought his own four battalions up against the Marathas, who made a precipitate retreat into the marsh, where many perished, including two of Holkar's principal officers.

At the same time the 3rd Brigade, under Lieut.-Colonel Ball, arrived on the scene and proceeded to secure the captured guns and carry the British wounded into a place of safety. In this task the 3rd Brigade was assisted by the two native cavalry regiments, under Lieut.-Colonel T. Brown, who had covered the advance of the infantry at the beginning of the battle and had successfully held off the large mounted force of the Marathas throughout the day's fighting. This performance was a remarkable one, for Lieut.-Colonel Brown had only 484 sabres in action in his two regiments.

The British force encamped on the field of battle, their front guarded by a cavalry picquet on the rising ground near the first Maratha position, and about half-way between the British camp and the fortress of Dig.

The battle of Dig was won entirely by hard fighting. General Fraser's wound proving mortal, he was unable to write any despatch, and it is therefore impossible to say what his precise intentions were regarding the conduct of the fight. The Marathas' position, however, was unassailable save by a frontal attack, and the resolution having been formed to make this attack, it would appear that Monson performed his task bravely and well.

An unfriendly critic has stated that General Fraser's plans for the battle were admirable, and that, after his fall, Monson made no attempt to carry them out, neglecting to make use of his native troops and concerning himself only with leading the 76th and Bengal Europeans. There appears to be little, if any, truth in this accusation, and Monson must be considered fortunate in obtaining this opportunity of regaining his military reputation, and in having made a good use of it.

The British casualties in the battle of Dig were very severe, amounting to 643, including 21 officers. The Maratha losses were, however, much heavier, it being believed that nearly 2000 were either killed or drowned in attempting to effect their escape.

The captured guns numbered 87, and among them were 14 guns and 1 howitzer which had been captured in Monson's retreat. There were also six 18-pounders, presented in 1792 to the Marathas at Seringapatam, they being then our allies—an interesting token of the shifting conditions of Indian policy at this period.

In Brigadier-General Monson's report on the battle of Dig, the mentions of officers were confined to commanding officers and the staff. When forwarding the report to the Governor-General, General Lake generously stated his opinion that the victory surpassed anything that had previously been done in India, and expressed his belief that, in conjunction with his own defeat of Holkar, it had practically ended the war.

Monson unhappily displayed his fatal want of judgment immediately after the victory, writing to Lake that he intended to fall back on Muttra for supplies. Lake justly commented on this proposal that, as there were ample supplies at Muttra, Monson should have drawn them from there, for which purpose he could easily have detached two regiments after his victory: to fall back from Dig would be looked upon by the natives as tantamount to a retreat.

Monson's retirement was indeed a glaring error, for which there was no excuse. It enabled some of Holkar's army to escape and other portions to enter Dig, and it gave the necessary encouragement to Holkar to continue the war.

General Lake, who had left Fatehgarh on November 20, hurried to Muttra to take over charge of the army before Monson could do any worse mischief, and arrived there on the 28th.

The Raja of Bhartpur, to whom Dig belonged, was now an open foe, instead of a treacherous ally. He had, as already stated, concluded a treaty with the British Government after the battle of Delhi, by which the possession of his territories had been guaranteed to him. He had, moreover, subsequently received, as a free gift, lands nearly equal in value to one-third of his original possessions. The Raja, almost immediately after the conclusion of the treaty, entered into a secret correspondence with Holkar, and during the retreat of Monson's detachment showed his intentions more boldly. The climax was reached during the battle of Dig, when a party of Bhartpur horse took an active share in the fighting, and the fortress, which belonged to the Raja, opened fire on our infantry as they were capturing the positions held by Holkar's troops. General Lake therefore decided to use his discretionary powers and to commence immediate operations against the Raja, in anticipation of the Governor-General's approval. Lord Mornington, on December 20, formally approved of General Lake's proceedings, but Dig had fallen some days before the arrival of his despatch.

Lake had advanced from Muttra on December 1, moving towards Dig, the garrison of which place had been raised to great strength by the inclusion of a portion of Holkar's infantry and a number of his guns, which had escaped capture in the battle of November 13. On December 2 the army encamped in sight of Dig, and halted for nine days, pending the arrival of the reserve brigade and a small battering-train, which were marching from Agra under Lieut.-Colonel Don. During the halt General Lake moved out repeatedly to reconnoitre the country about Dig, on which occasions Holkar's cavalry showed considerable boldness.

The troops arrived from Agra on December 10, and on the following day the army marched in two columns 600 yards apart. The intermediate space was occupied by the artillery, baggage, and provision train; the reserve brigade formed an advanced-guard; and the picquets, strengthened by a regiment of cavalry, formed a rear-guard. The camp-followers were still inordinately numerous, and in the great square, formed as described, there marched, writes Thorn, "not less than 60,000 human beings, 200 elephants, 2000 camels, and 100,000 bullocks, at a very moderate estimate."

The army encamped near the fortified village of Kasba Au, and on December 13 proceeded, in the same order of march as on the 11th, to the position selected by the Commander-in-Chief for his attack on the fortress. The ground selected for the encampment lay to the west of the town of Dig, which was of considerable size, the circuit of the walls being 4¾ miles. The town was surrounded by lofty walls, with round bastions connected by earthen ramparts. Within the town was a citadel of about 150 yards square, with ramparts 70 to 100 feet high and 20 to 50 feet thick, surrounded by a wet ditch. At the time of the attack the town walls mounted thirty-one guns of all sizes, from 74-pounders to 4-pounders. The point chosen for attack was the south-west angle, which is formed by a small enclosed work called the Shah Burj, about 50 yards square, having an exposed masonry wall 36 feet high, which could be breached from a distance. Five hundred yards south of this is a detached work called Gopal Garh.

Having taken up his position, General Lake immediately opened his trenches against the fortress, the reserve, under Colonel Don, first driving the Marathas from the grove of trees from which it was desired to commence operations. The Pioneers, under Captain Swinton and Lieutenant Forrest, immediately broke ground, and worked so quickly through the night that before daylight they had completed a small parallel 300 yards long, and two small batteries.

On the evening of December 14 volunteers from the three British cavalry regiments began the construction of a breaching battery within 750 yards of the Shall Burj. This battery was within easy range of the detached fort of Gopal Garh, which was crowded with matchlock-men, whose fire greatly annoyed the working parties. Lake was apparently bent on his main object, the capture of the entire fortress, and would not spare the time that would have been taken up by the previous capture of Gopal Garh.

The work on the breaching battery was therefore hurried on, and it was able to open fire with fourteen guns on the morning of December 17. Their fire, however, proved very ineffectual, and on the 20th a second battery, at even closer range, was erected, in order to bring a crossfire on the breach. The Marathas, on their part, had used their guns with considerable skill, and had managed to enfilade both the British batteries, until Colonel Horsford silenced their fire by distributing his own guns in several localities about the plain. The author of *A Military Autobiography* says that the enemy were throwing shells which, as they were known to have come into their hands during the retreat on Agra, were greeted whenever they burst with cries of "Thank you, Colonel Monson!"

Beside the reinforcement which they had afforded to the garrison of Dig, part of Holkar's infantry were entrenched outside the walls, and also held the ravines near the British attack, thus adding greatly to the difficulties of the operations.

At length a practicable breach was reported, an assault was ordered, and at half-past eleven on the night of December 23 a storming -party moved down to the trenches. The force detailed for the assault was divided into three columns. The right column, consisting of four companies of the Bengal European Regiment and five companies 1st Battalion 12th Native Infantry, under Captain Kelly, was ordered to carry the enemy's batteries outside the fortress, between the Shah Biirj and Gopal Garh—that is, on the right of the main attack. The left column, composed of a like number of companies of the same regiments, under Major Radcliffe, was to carry the entrenchments and batteries on the left of the main attack. The centre column, led by Lieut.-Colonel Macrae, consisting of the flank companies of the 22nd, 76th, and Bengal European regiments and the 1st Battalion 8th Native Infantry, was to storm the breach in the Shah Biirj.

The centre column found the plain under the breach so covered with the debris of the broken walls that its progress in the darkness was seriously impeded. The outer columns consequently came into action first, springing into the enemy's outworks, which they soon succeeded in capturing, forcing the enemy to seek cover within the fortress, and securing the guns, which they spiked.

In the meantime Macrae's column, having with great difficulty crossed the plain, formed up for the attack under cover of the walls of the fortress, and the order to storm having been given by Macrae, a rush was made up the incline. The leading files, scrambling over the broken masonry, gained the breach, when there ensued a desperate fight for its possession. The first few men who forced their way through the breach were sabred by the enemy; but the rest of the column quickly followed, and, favoured by the darkness, flocked through the breach, and charging forward, carried the southwest bastion of the Shah Biirj. The enemy's artillerymen showed great courage and determination, fighting with their *tulwars* against the bayonets of our soldiers, until at last, overpowered, they lay in mangled heaps around their guns.

One of the first to mount the breach was Charles Metcalfe, afterwards Lord Metcalfe, then a young civilian aged nineteen, who had been despatched from Calcutta by Lord Wellesley to act as civil *attaché* to the Commander-in-Chief. It is believed that some of the officers of Lake's staff had resented the presence of a civil officer in the field, and that Metcalfe took this opportunity of showing his martial instincts. General Lake mentioned Metcalfe's gallantry in his despatch, and ever after spoke of him as "my young stormer." Metcalfe was the nephew by marriage of Colonel Monson, his mother being the sister of Mrs Monson.

Kelly's and Radcliffe's columns now joined Macrae in

the captured bastion; and having re-formed, the united force attacked the main walls of the fortress to the south and west, most of the bastions being carried at the point of the bayonet.

The British column now formed up inside the walls and advanced towards the gate of the citadel. Preparations were made for its capture, and Lieutenant G. Pollock, Bengal Artillery, was detailed to blow in the gate. Some unavoidable delay occurred before the citadel could be assaulted, and its garrison, who had been alarmed by the determined attack of our troops on the Shah Biirj, took advantage of the respite afforded them and stole secretly away during the night of December 24, making for Bhartpur. Thus on Christmas morning, after a siege of twelve days, Dig was in General Lake's hands.

The cost of the operations was by no means heavy, the killed numbering 4 officers and 39 men; 13 officers and 171 men were wounded. Captain Effingham Lindsay, who commanded the flank companies of the 22nd, received two wounds, and three of his subalterns were wounded. Among other casualties in the 22nd was Sergeant Shipp, of whom we shall hear more.

The capture of Dig appears to have been, in a considerable measure, due to the neglect of the Marathas to repair the breach in the Shah Biirj prior to the assault. Their neglect to do so is probably attributable to over-confidence in the strong works outside the fortress, which might well have been expected to hold their own against the weak flanking columns of assault.

The British-Indian infantry, indeed, showed very fine fighting quality in the assault at Dig, and the easy triumph which resulted contributed, with that at Aligarh, to encourage General Lake in his belief that his army, if boldly led, could achieve any capture. For this belief he was, unfortunately, soon to suffer.

In his despatch General Lake laid special stress on the good services of Colonel Horsford and the artillery, thanking also the leaders of the three columns of assault, and in addition, Lieut.-Colonel Ball of the 1st Battalion 8th Native Infantry, Captain Lindsay of the 22nd Regiment, and Captain Robertson and Lieutenant Smith of the Engineers. Both of the officers of Pioneers, Captain Swinton and Lieutenant Forrest, were severely wounded during the operations, Lieutenant Forrest sustaining twenty-one wounds. He was left on the ground for dead, but recovered with the loss of an arm.

One hundred guns were captured at Dig, and the loss of life among the Jats and Marathas was great.

John Shipp states in his memoirs that when the British army marched into Dig they found five companies of sepoys who had deserted during Colonel Monson's retreat. The sepoys, wearing the uniform in which they had deserted, stood "outside the principal gate of the fort, with their arms ordered, without apparently making any resistance, and frequently crying out, 'Englishmen, Englishmen, pray do not kill us; for God's sake do not kill us.' As these supplications," continues the worthy Shipp, " proceeded rather from fear than from penitence for the crime they had been guilty of—that of deserting to an enemy— these men could expect no mercy. We had positive orders to give them no quarter, and they were most of them shot." The order to give no quarter was probably directed against the garrison of Hinglazgarh, who are said by Colonel Skinner to have entered Holkar's service.

General Lake left the 1st Battalion 4th Native Infantry in garrison and marched from Dig for Bhartpur on December 28. He was joined on the 31st, while on the march thither, by Major-General Dowdeswell with the

75th Regiment and a convoy of stores. After this rein-forcement the strength of the army was about 7800 men, thus composed:

British cavalry	800
Native cavalry	1600
British infantry	1000
Native infantry	4400

The Engineer department was represented by three officers and three companies of Pioneers, each under an infantry officer. The ordnance comprised 61 guns and 18 howitzers and mortars, manned by 15 officers and 200 European artillerymen, with about 800 native gun-*lascars* and *golundaz*, part of whom had recently joined from Sindhia's service. Of the 61 guns, only six 18-pounders were heavy enough for siege operations.

With this weak and ill-equipped force General Lake had to choose between two tasks, for either of which it was inadequate. He could either leave the Raja of Bhartpur to be dealt with subsequently and devote his energies to the pursuit of Holkar, or he might decide to attack Bhartpur, and so, by its capture and that of the remaining strongholds in that state, which were of no strength, deprive Holkar of his last-remaining footing in Hindustan, and ensure his eventual destruction.

Lake, as we already know, had decided on the second course. His cavalry were for the time in no condition to undertake another rapid pursuit of Holkar, and Skinner had been despatched to Aligarh to raise more irregulars. These could not take the field for a couple of months at any rate, and Lake therefore decided to utilise this period by the capture of Bhartpur. He apparently felt no doubt of his ability to perform this task, in spite of the weakness of his army and the inadequacy of his siege artillery, and the history of the war justified him in his confidence. Aligarh, Agra, and

Gwalior were among the strongest fortresses in India, and, until the coming of Lake, had been considered impregnable; yet Aligarh had been captured in a morning, and Agra and Gwalior had surrendered to avoid a storm. Dig, also a powerful and strongly garrisoned town, had just fallen a very easy prey to his arms. Lake cannot be fairly blamed for believing that he would be equally successful at Bhartpur.

Lake therefore began the New Year by marching confidently forward, his army as light-hearted as himself, and on January 2, 1805, he encamped about two miles south-west of Bhartpur. The march had been a long and tedious one, and the troops therefore gladly rested on the following day, while the quartermasters' establishments of the various corps were employed in collecting materials for fascines and gabions, and in constructing them under the superintendence of Lieutenant Robertson, the senior officer of Engineers.

The fortress of Bhartpur, now to become famous, stands upon a plain amidst jungle and water, and is distant about thirty miles W.N.W. of Agra. The town has a perimeter of about five miles, and in 1805 was surrounded by an immense mud wall of very rude design, but practically impervious to artillery fire. Outside the wall was a wet ditch of varying depth. The garrison is believed to have amounted to 50,000 men, amply provided with food and military stores: large numbers of guns were mounted on the bastions, and Holkar was outside, with a large force, to hamper the besieging army. The point of attack having already been chosen, the encampment was located so as to face it, and on the evening of January 3 a party of infantry with two guns, under Lieut.-Colonel Maitland, 75th Regiment, occupied a garden surrounded by a low mud wall, distant about 1200 yards from the wall of Bhartpur. From this garden one bastion, with part of the ramparts, was visible, the view elsewhere being obstructed by dense jungle. About 500 yards in advance of this garden, or 700 yards from the rampart, a breaching battery for six 18-pounders was constructed. On either side of it, and about 400 yards apart, two small fortified posts were constructed, in order to protect the battery from enfilade fire from the adjoining jungle. The battery opened fire early on January 7, work having been pushed forward with the utmost haste; but as it had been built entirely of brushwood, and constructed so hastily, the fire was therefore not directed on the exact point of the curtain that it had been intended to breach. The point of attack being now made evident, the enemy occupied positions outside the walls from which they could bring a flanking fire on any attacking force, and also deepened the ditch in front of the incipient breach.

During the night of the 7th trenches were dug connecting the battery with the two flanking posts, and eight mortars were placed on the right of the battery.

On January 8 the augmented battery opened fire on the town and on the enemy's posts outside the ditch, as well as on the breach, which was reported practicable in the course of the day. Efforts were also made, but without effect, to prevent the enemy from stockading and repairing the breach during the night following, on which the Cornmander-in-Chief intended to assault. On January 9, therefore, the breaching battery kept up a heavy fire all day, until at dusk the troops told off for the storming-party went to the front and compelled a cessation of the fire. The stormers were thus distributed:

Main Attack
> Lieut.-Colonel Maitland, 75th Regiment, commanding
> Flank Companies of the 22nd, 75th, 76th, and Bengal European Regiments—in all about 500 men.
> 1st Battalion 8th and 2nd Battalion 12th Native Infantry
> Four 6-pounders

Right Attack
Major Hawkes commanding
Two Companies 75th Regiment
1st Battalion 2nd Native Infantry
Two 6-pounders

Left Attack
Lieut.-Colonel Rayne commanding
100 men of the Bengal European Regiment
2nd Battalion 22nd Native Infantry
Two 6-pounders

The main attack was headed by a forlorn-hope of twelve European volunteers, led by Sergeant Shipp, 22nd Regiment, who had been severely wounded at Dig. The orders to Major Hawkes were to attack the enemy's position near the Anah gate, and afterwards the gate itself. Should this prove impossible, he was to move to his left and proceed down to support the main attack. In like manner, Lieut.-Colonel Rayne was ordered to attack the Kumbhir gate, and if possible to carry it: he was also to support the main attack.

The ground between their starting-point and the places they were ordered to attack had not been examined by any of the leaders of columns, nor were they provided with guides. The ground traversed was broken, and in many places there were deep pools of water. It is therefore almost a matter of surprise that any of them reached their objective. That the attack failed can cause no surprise whatever.

The right column was the most successful, for Major Hawkes found the position before the Anah gate, captured it at the point of the bayonet, and spiked three of the guns. Instead, however, of carrying out his orders to attack the gate, he then proceeded to join the main attack. Lieut.-Colonel Rayne failed to reach the Kumbhir gate, and was compelled to return. As for the main attack, a part only of the column reached the ditch. The flank companies of the 22nd Regiment did, however, succeed in arriving at a point opposite the breach, and a party of twenty-three men, under Lieutenant Manser, crossed the ditch, though the water was breast-high. Lieutenant Manser ordered his men to sit down under cover, while he went in search of the rest of the column.

The whole main attack, with the finest courage, gradually closed on the point of attack, and Lieut.-Colonel Maitland showed desperate determination, repeatedly leading small parties of men forward to the attack. After receiving several wounds, he was at last shot through the head and instantaneously killed near the top of the breach. In these efforts Maitland was seconded by many devoted officers; but such isolated attacks could by no possibility succeed, and merely caused a fruitless loss of life. The defenders of Bhartpur had stockaded the breach, and during the attack and the subsequent retirement poured a terrific fire on the British columns while themselves in perfect safety. The first assault consequently failed with heavy loss, the killed numbering 4 officers and 96 men, and the wounded 23 officers and 341 men. The losses of the Europeans were very heavy, particularly in the flank companies of the 22nd and 75th Regiments, which latter regiment had its commanding officer killed and 8 officers wounded. As only four companies of the regiment were engaged, it appears that most of the officers employed were killed or wounded.

Disastrous as this attempt had proved, Lake and his army neither lost confidence nor slackened their efforts. On the contrary, two new batteries were constructed, in one of which were placed four 18-pounders and two fresh 24-pounders, brought over from Dig. Fire was concentrated on a portion of the curtain to the right of the bastion between the Anah and Kumbhir gates, the previous breach having been to the left of that bastion. The new breach was consequently nearer the Anah gate than the old one.

On this breach the guns kept up a fairly heavy fire from January 15 to 20, and many shells were thrown into the town, causing a number of casualties among the crowded defenders. Among the slain was a brother of the Raja, who was killed while looking at the British dead lying in the old breach by a single aimed shell fired by Captain Nelly of the Bengal Artillery; and the eldest son of the Raja was also wounded in the arm by a chance shot.

On January 18 Major-General Smith joined the army with three battalions of Native Infantry and 100 European convalescents—in all, about 1600 men. General Smith, like Lake, had been an officer of the First Guards, in which regiment he served twenty-five years. He had also served under Lake in the campaign of 1793-94 in the Netherlands. Ismail Beg, an independent chief in Holkar's army, also joined the British, bringing with him 500 of his followers. On the other hand, the Raja of Bhartpur, who possessed great wealth, bought the alliance of Amir Khan by a gift of six *lakhs* of rupees.

In view of a renewed assault, it was felt that a reconnaissance of the ground up to the ditch and an examination of the ditch itself were necessary. A reconnaissance in force was at first contemplated, but as this would have entailed a heavy loss of life, an offer made by some volunteers was accepted. On January 20 a havildar and three troopers of the 3rd Bengal Cavalry, under pretence of being deserters, rode down to the ditch pursued and fired at by a party of sepoys. The horsemen succeeded in reaching the ditch and in riding along it as far as the Anah gate, but the reconnaissance thus effected was too hurried to be trustworthy. They reported that the new breach was practicable, and that the ditch in front of it was 28 feet wide and not deep. Three ladders, covered with laths and broad enough to carry two men abreast, had been prepared to act as floating ditches, and on this favourable report an assault was ordered for the following morning. On this occasion the troops detailed for the attack were taken into the trenches before daylight on January 21, with orders to advance about noon or whenever the batteries should have been able to destroy any repairs that the Marathas might have effected at the breach. This took longer than was expected, and it was not until 3 p.m. that the attacking force left the trenches. It was divided into two columns—the right, under Lieut.-Colonel Simpson, having orders to attack the Anah gate; and the left, commanded by Lieut.-Colonel Macrae, 75th Regiment, being ordered to storm the breach.

Lieut.-Colonel Macrae's column was headed by the following parties from the four British regiments: 120 of the 75th, 150 of the 76th, 100 of the First Bengal Europeans, and 50 of the flank companies of the 22nd. This party was led by Captain Lindsay of the 22nd, who had been severely wounded at the assault of Dig, but now threw away his crutch and marched with his left arm in a sling.

In support of the British detachments followed the 2nd Battalion 15th and the 2nd Battalion 22nd Native Infantry, and four 6-pounder guns, while the remainder of the 75th and 76th Regiments were ordered to form a covering party and to keep down the fire from the ramparts during the assault. A picked body of Europeans carried the portable bridges, in the use of which they had been practiced, and the scaling-ladders were entrusted to a party of native pioneers.

Lieut.-Colonel Macrae moved straight on the breach, and on reaching a dry tank some 200 yards from it, he halted his column under cover of the bank and went forward himself with the bridges, scaling-ladders, and a small party of Europeans. On reaching the ditch, Macrae found that instead of being 28 feet it was 40 feet across. An attempt was made to lengthen the bridges by lashing scaling-ladders to them, but this failed. Lieutenant Morris, with some men of the Bengal European Regiment, swam the ditch and mounted the breach, Morris being twice wounded; but it was evident that no assault was possible, and Lieut.-Colonel Macrae wisely ordered a retirement.

The right column meanwhile had reached the Anah gate, but failed to force it, and Lieut.-Colonel Simpson therefore united with the main column and assisted to carry away the four 6-pounders, which had gallantly come into action in the opening close to the breach and had suffered some loss. The second assault on Bhartpur was thus as complete a failure as the first, and for the same reason—insufficient reconnaissance prior to the assault. On this occasion the breach was found practicable, and had more care been taken to ascertain how the ditch could be bridged, the assault would probably have succeeded.

The casualties among the Europeans were 18 officers and 284 men killed and wounded, and there were 285 casualties in the native regiments engaged. The European portion of the main column, being in front, suffered terribly. Of the 50 men of the 22nd, 41 were killed or wounded, and the gallant Sergeant Shipp, who led as usual, was dangerously wounded. The 120 of the 75th lost 111, the 150 of the 76th lost 75, and the 100 Bengal Europeans lost 40. Nearly all the officers of the European detachments were killed or wounded. The gallant Captain Lindsay of the 22nd lost his leg; the 75th had three officers wounded; and the 76th, already so cruelly reduced, had two officers killed and three wounded. The enemy disgraced themselves by barbarously murdering all the wounded who could not be carried away.

This massacre took place in full view of the British trenches, and seriously affected the moral of the army.

Amir Khan had now appeared on the scenes, and while the second assault was in progress the whole plain in rear of Lake's army was covered by his cavalry and that of Holkar and the Bhartpur Raja. Lake, with his cavalry and horse artillery, moved out to cover the camp, and inflicted some loss on the enemy; but the British camp was for a time as much besieged as was Bhartpur itself.

Lake published a General Order warmly thanking the troops engaged in the second assault for their gallantry and steadiness, and assuring the army of his confidence that, in a very few days, this good conduct and courage would be rewarded by the possession of Bhartpur.

After the failure of the second assault the army lay inactive before the fortress for a considerable time. It was necessary to select an easier point of attack, and at first there was also a scarcity of supplies. General Lake was also watching for an opportunity of dealing a blow at Holkar and Amir Khan.

While efforts were being made to find a weak point in the defences of Bhartpur, two convoys were despatched, from Muttra and Agra respectively, carrying provisions to the army. The Muttra convoy, of 12,000 bullocks, guarded by a few matchlock-men, was met on January 22 by the 1st Bengal Cavalry and the 1st Battalion 15th Native Infantry, under Captain Walsh of the former corps—an insufficient force for the purpose. Amir Khan, hearing of the weakness of Walsh's detachment, attacked him on the march at the head of 8,000 horse and foot, with four guns. Captain Walsh took post in a village and defended as much of the convoy as he could collect, but was about to be crushed by superior numbers when rescued by Lieut.-Colonel Need, at the head of the 27th Light Dragoons and the 2nd Bengal Cavalry. The gallant escort, seeing the dust raised by Need's regiments, imagined that General Lake, with all the cavalry, was coming to their rescue, and were so animated as to sally forth from their village and make a vigorous bayonet charge on Amir Khan's infantry, 600 of whom were killed, being deserted by their cavalry. Amir Khan himself narrowly escaped capture, getting away on foot and in disguise. Of the 12,000 bullock-loads of grain, however, but 1800 reached the army. It is to be regretted that Captain Walsh, when he saw the cavalry coming to his assistance, could not refrain from exclaiming, "A friend in need is a friend indeed."

On the day after this affair, General Lake despatched a strong escort of three regiments of cavalry and three battalions of infantry under Lieut.-Colonel Patrick Don to Agra, to guard the second convoy, which was a very large and important one, consisting of 50,000 bullocks carrying grain, 800 bullock-carts of stores and ammunition (including 8000 rounds of 18-pounder shot for the breaching battery), and six *lakhs* of rupees. This immense convoy left Agra on January 28, and proved an irresistible bait to Amir Khan and his allies.

Holkar, Amir Khan, and Bapuji Sindhia all sallied forth with a large force of infantry and every mounted man they had at their command. When this force, formidable at least in numbers, was well away from Bhartpur, Lake fearlessly pursued them with the remainder of his cavalry and two battalions of infantry. The enemy were so alarmed at finding themselves between the convoy and Lake's force, that far from endeavouring to capture the convoy, they sheered off to a respectful distance, and the convoy was eventually brought into camp without the loss of a bullock.

The Raja of Bhartpur now saw that he was getting a very poor return for the six *lakhs* of rupees that he had given to Amir Khan, and taunted the latter with his failure. Amir Khan, who had relied on filling his pockets, and had lost both men and reputation instead of so doing, was also discontented. He therefore determined to make a raid into Rohilkhand, his native country, thinking that he would there obtain ample plunder, and that Lake could not spare troops to pursue him. He had good reason to suppose so, but little knew Lake's dauntless courage and determination.

Amir Khan therefore left the allied army and crossed the Jumna on February 7 with his whole mounted force and as many of Holkar's irregulars as were willing to accompany him. Lake, on the following day, despatched Major-General Smith in pursuit with the Horse Artillery, the three British cavalry regiments, and the 1st, 3rd, and 6th Bengal Cavalry. Charles Metcalfe accompanied General Smith as political adviser, and rendered valuable services. Amir Khan's raid was entirely frustrated, for Major-General Smith's force followed him so closely through the Doab that he had no time for operations against the large towns, which alone were worth robbing.

On passing Aligarh (February 11), General Smith picked up Captain Skinner with 500 of his horse, who did excellent service. During the pursuit the whole British force forded the Ganges at a point where it was nearly a mile wide, though the stream, at the time of crossing, was not more than half that width.

On arriving at Moradabad (February 18) the cavalry found Mr Leycester, the collector, gallantly defending his house, which he had converted into a miniature fortress. Aided by the local residents and their servants and a few militia, Mr Leycester had successfully repulsed several assaults, when General Smith's force fortunately came up and prevented an inevitable disaster.

After a long and pertinacious pursuit throughout eastern Rohilkhand, General Smith at last succeeded in bringing Amir Khan to action on March 2 at Afzalgarh.

The British force—from which was deducted the 3rd Bengal Cavalry, left in charge of the baggage—numbered about 1400 regular cavalry, with Skinner's 500 irregulars in addition. It came up with Amir Khan's force at two in the afternoon, and found it drawn up in order of battle, with the Ramgunga river in its front and the Kumaon hills in the rear.

The small British force, having forded the river, was formed up in two lines—the first consisting of the 27th and 29th Light Dragoons; and the second, of the 8th Light Dragoons and the 6th Bengal Cavalry. Skinner's horse were ordered to guard the left, and the 1st Bengal Cavalry the right flank, but there was not time to complete this disposition. As the first line advanced from the river the enemy advanced also, on which the Horse Artillery went to the front and opened a brisk fire. At this moment about 500 of the enemy's Rohilla horsemen suddenly charged, and the General, seeing his artillery imperilled, ordered the 27th Light Dragoons to advance through the guns and repel them.

Barely had the 27th passed through the guns when the Rohillas were upon them, and taking them thus at the walk, drove them back in confusion on the guns. Captain Brown was unable to fire into the mingled mass of friend and foe, and a disaster seemed imminent, when the prompt action of a squadron leader saved the day. Captain George Deare, whose squadron of the 8th Light Dragoons was on the right flank of the second line, advanced, and wheeling to the left, charged down the front and drove off the Rohillas in headlong flight.

While the frontal attack was thus repulsed, those made on either flank of the British force also failed, Skinner's horse charging with great effect on the left, while on the right the fire of the galloper guns proved highly effective.

The loss of the British was not more than forty killed and wounded, but Amir Khan's force was severely punished. A number of his best officers were killed, and a body of his Rohilla countrymen, who had joined him and fought very courageously as infantry, fell almost to a man. On March 5 Major-General Smith's force arrived at Moradabad, and found that Amir Khan had passed by the town on the previous day.

Leaving his wounded, Smith marched to Bareilly in order to protect southern Rohilkhand from the marauder. Two other British detachments were now in the field farther north, Colonel Burn having come down from Saharunpur, and a mounted force under Captain Murray acting in co-operation with him. The latter force inflicted a severe defeat on Amir Khan on March 8, at Chandpur, near Amroha. The result of these movements was that Amir Khan suddenly abandoned Rohilkhand, re-crossing the Ganges and making his way to Bhartpur, whence he presently departed to Bundelkhand. Major-General Smith followed him to Bhartpur, rejoining the army there on March 23 after an effective pursuit of over 700 miles in forty-four days—a noteworthy exploit for an infantry general.

During his absence two more attempts had been made to storm the fortress.

General Lake had decided that the strength of the Kumbhir and Anah gates, and the depth of the portion of the ditch lying between them, rendered further attacks in that quarter impossible, and on information that there was much less water farther east, he decided to take up fresh ground in that direction. This was also desirable for sanitary reasons, so on February 6 the army changed position, encamping with its left nearly opposite the Anah gate and its right facing the Nimdar gate.

It was determined to breach between the two bastions nearest to the Anah gate.

A grave oversight was the neglect to capture an advanced post on some rising ground opposite the Nimdar gate. A battery was constructed to fire on the post, but it cannot be doubted it should have been taken before any attempt was made to attack Bhartpur itself from this quarter.

On February 11 the army received a considerable accession of strength from the arrival in camp of the Bombay column, formerly commanded by Colonel Murray. This officer had been removed from his command in consequence of his failure to assist Colonel Monson, and the column was now commanded by Major-General Richard Jones of the Bombay Artillery. Great interest was felt by the Bengal army in this meeting with Bombay troops, whose appearance was jealously scanned. The Bombay men had been five years on active service, and it was generally admitted by candid spectators that they had a business-like look. They carried much less baggage with them than did the troops of Bengal. There was a fine emulation between the troops of the two Presidencies,— the Bombay men requesting that as newcomers they might be given the next chance of action, while the Bengal troops, worn as they were, begged to be allowed to finish off their work.

They had, indeed, shown the utmost zeal and cheerfulness in trying conditions, and the officers and men of the Bengal European Regiment, good fighters all, had been conspicuous for their exertions in the trenches. The Commander-in-Chief, who personally supervised the fieldworks, frequently thanked them for their hard work, and on one occasion (says the regimental history) some of the men of the regiment apologised to the Chief for their dirty appearance, urging as an excuse that they had not found time to change their shirts for several weeks. General Lake

175

remarked approvingly that their dirty shirts were an honour to the wearers, showing that they had willingly sacrificed comfort to duty; and his Excellency used frequently to address the regiment as his own "Dirty Shirts,"—a name which was treasured with pride by the Bengal regiment ever afterwards. Some handsome pieces of plate on the mess-table of that famous old corps are inscribed as the gift of "An old Dirty Shirt." Major General Jones' force consisted of:

1 Troop Bombay Cavalry
500 Irregular Horse
65th Regiment (8 companies)
86th Regiment
2nd Battalion 1st Bombay Native Infantry
2nd Battalion 2nd Bombay Native Infantry
1st Battalion 3rd Bombay Native Infantry
1st Battalion 9th Bombay Native Infantry
Two 12-pounders
Twelve 6-pounders
Two field howitzers

In all, about 700 Europeans and 2400 native cavalry and infantry.

The batteries had now been at work for several days, and on the day on which the Bombay troops arrived the new breach was reported practicable. The mistake of breaching before the arrangements for assault were complete was thus repeated.

On this same night a trench leading up to the bastion nearest the Anah gate was commenced, while on their part the enemy not only stockaded the breach but built a mud wall in support of the stockade. The enemy's artillery fire was unsubdued, and our gunners now found Lake's punctilio in regard to uniform highly inconvenient, for whenever the General and his staff visited the trenches their scarlet coats and plumed hats brought down a shower of shot. This continued until a plain-spoken captain of artillery told George Lake that his feathers endangered the life of every man in the battery, and begged him to lay them aside when he came down there,—a request that was afterwards complied with by all the staff.

The third assault was ordered to be made on February 20, and there was now a sufficient force for the purpose; but a fatal want of care regarding details marred the design. A sufficient number of troops was not kept in the approaches, and this fact becoming known to the enemy, a daring and successful sortie was made from Bhartpur early on the morning of .February 19. On this occasion the assailants, accompanied by coolies and women (a fact which shows how thoroughly they knew the state of affairs in the British approaches), made their way to a newly constructed battery and destroyed it, emptying and carrying away the sand-bags.

Such an incident should surely have prevented an opportunity being given for another surprise, but on the following morning—the very day on which the assault was ordered—a general sortie was made from the town, and the whole of the trenches were attacked. The scene was a curious one. The enemy ran along the crest of the trenches, aiming blows with their spears and swords at the troops crowded below them in the trenches, and awaiting the order to assault. The bold assailants were eventually cleared off by the flank companies of the 22nd, whose conduct was conspicuous on every occasion, and the British batteries opened fire on the defences that had been constructed in the breach.

The troops for the assault had been formed in three columns, as follows:

Right Column
   Lieut.-Colonel Taylor
   65th Regiment, 300 men
   1st Grenadier Battalion Bombay Native Infantry
   1st Battalion 3rd Bombay Native Infantry

Centre Column
   Captain Grant, 86th Regiment
   86th Regiment, 200 men
   1st Battalion 8th Bengal Native Infantry

Left Column
   Lieut.-Colonel Patrick Don
   22nd Regiment.
   75th Regiment
   76th Regiment
   Bengal European Regiment
   1st Battalion 12th Bengal Native Infantry
   2nd Battalion 12th Bengal Native Infantry
   1st Battalion 15th Bengal Native Infantry

Of these, the right and centre columns were destined to make auxiliary attacks, while the strong left column was to assault the breach.

The right column was ordered to make a detour far to the right and to force the Bhim Narayan gate, which was reported easy of access. The column was led by its guide under the fire of the town, lost its scaling-ladders, and had a 12-pounder gun dismounted. It was then ordered to return to camp. The centre column carried out its orders successfully. Advancing at 3 p.m., the hour named for the assault, it advanced and carried the high ground opposite the Nimdar gate, capturing eleven guns and pursuing the enemy up to the Atil gate, which was only closed as the head of the column reached it. For a moment it appeared as if Grant and his little column would actually effect an entrance, and Lake's ready expectation of success was aroused, but it was soon disappointed.

This success should have rendered the task of the assaulting column comparatively easy, but, sad to relate, the attack ignominiously failed on account of the misconduct of those very troops who had so often covered themselves with glory. The signal for the advance was the sound of the attack of the centre column, which was heard about 4 p.m. Fifty men of the main attack were then to approach the breach by way of the trench, which had been constructed to the very edge of the ditch: they were then to file outwards and open fire on the wall to the right and left of the breach, while the storming-party advanced to the attack.

The troops had now been waiting many hours in a hot sun. They had been considerably demoralised by the attack that had been made on them in the early morning, and yet more so by the fact that the extremity of the approach had remained all day in the hands of some of the enemy. Therefore, when the order to advance was given, the fascine bearers hesitated: a rumour spread that the approach had been mined, and the European troops in front finally refused to advance.

Lieut.-Colonel Don, grasping the situation, called on the troops in rear to quit the approach and follow him, whereupon the glorious remnant of the 22nd flank companies at once stepped out of the trench, as did the 12th Bengal Native Infantry. They were supported by two 6-pounders, under Lieutenant G. Swiney. Led by Don, these brave soldiers advanced on the bastion on the right of the breach, where the ditch was less deep. (A tall sepoy had already proved, by jumping into the water, that in front of the breach it was impassable.) A party of the 12th Native Infantry succeeded in clambering to the top of the bastion and there planted their regimental colour, and many individuals of this regiment and the surviving 22nd flankers showed great gallantry. So difficult of access was the bastion that the men had to climb up singly, some reaching the crest of the parapet, and some entering through the embrasures. In such circumstances success was impossible.

A chance was now, however, given, for, seeing the colour of the 12th Native Infantry on the bastion, the defenders of the breach thought that the storming-party must be near, and exploded the mines that had been prepared for its defence. Fourteen officers in the approach saw the opportunity, and running out, called on their men to follow them. Few, if any, answered to the appeal, and Colonel Don, seeing that the attempt was useless, recalled all who had gone on.

The losses in this disastrous affair were very heavy, amounting to 894. The native troops, who deserved all honour for their conduct, had 113 killed and 556 wounded. The Europeans had 49 killed and 176 wounded. Lake, in his despatch to Lord Wellesley, praised Captain Grant and his small column for their gallant conduct. While regretting the failure of the two other columns, he made no disparaging remarks as to the conduct of the troops, and assured the Governor-General that "though unfortunately not crowned with success, the exertions of Colonel Don were meritorious and gallant in the extreme."

General Lake, though much grieved by these heavy losses, and by the misconduct which had caused them and caused the failure of the assault, determined to make an immediate attempt to retrieve the prestige of his army. As it had been found practicable to clamber up the bastion on the right of the breach, it was thought that if heavily bombarded it might be rendered easy of access, and the battering guns were therefore turned on it. With the little ammunition that remained they made a large gap at the base of the bastion, but did not succeed in bringing it down.

Early the following morning (February 21) the European troops were formed up and, writes Thorn, addressed by Lake "in terms of affectionate regret, rather than stern severity." He expressed his sorrow that by not obeying their officers yesterday they had lost the laurels which they had gained on so many occasions. Being yet willing to give them an opportunity of retrieving their reputation, he now called for such as chose to volunteer for another effort to step out.

"Overpowered with shame and remorse," continues Thorn, "they all volunteered to a man; and Lieutenant Templeton, with a noble fervour of patriotic zeal, offered to lead the forlorn-hope." Templeton, one of the surviving officers of the 76th, had been wounded in the second assault. The storming-party, for the fourth and last attempt on Bhartpur, moved to the attack about three in the afternoon, led by Colonel Monson. It consisted of all the British infantry of the Bengal Division, and the 1st Battalion 2nd and 2nd Battalion 15th Bengal Native Infantry. The Bombay Division contributed the greater part of the 65th and 86th Regiments, the 1st Bombay Grenadier Battalion, and the flank companies of the 1st Battalion 3rd Bombay Native Infantry.

When the gallant remnant of the flank companies of the 22nd passed Lake, he was seen to turn away in tears. Quickly recovering himself, he waved his hat and cheered the brave fellows. As the stormers, cheering Lake, approached the breach, the ground was found strewn with the dead and wounded from the last assault, many stripped naked, some without heads, some without legs and arms, others shamefully mutilated and literally cut to pieces. Many of the poor fellows were still alive, and raised their heads, clotted with blood, others their legs and arms, making signs or faintly begging to be put out of their misery.

Undeterred by this horrible sight, the stormers, headed by Templeton and Shipp, moved steadily on to the bastion, which they endeavoured to climb. Some of the men, driving their bayonets into the rampart, endeavoured to gain a footing step by step; some clambered up by the shot-holes. The enemy, in great strength, defended the bastion and breach in the most determined way, keeping up an incessant shower of grape on our troops. The people on the walls, too, continually threw down upon them pieces of timber, flaming packs of cotton soaked in oil, solid shots, pots filled with gunpowder, and other explosives. The stormers showed the most determined courage, and maintained the struggle for two hours, when Monson, who had strained every nerve to attain success, reluctantly ordered a retirement.

The losses in this assault numbered 987, the European troops having 69 killed and 410 wounded. The native troops lost 56 killed and 452 wounded. Among the officers killed was the gallant Templeton, who fell just as he planted a Union-Jack flag on the bastion. Major Menzies, aide-de-camp to the Commander-in-Chief, was killed near the top of the breach. General Lake's attempts to storm Bhartpur thus finally failed, with a total loss of 103 officers and 3100 men.

In his despatch to Lord Wellesley he speaks in high terms of the "uncommon gallantry and perseverance" shown by Colonel Monson. Of the storming column he writes:

> Though the troops were unable to effect their object, I am happy to assure your lordship that they have on no occasion displayed greater steadiness. Those of the Bengal army supported their former character, and the Bombay division displayed a degree of resolution and discipline which entitles them to my highest praise and approbation.

In the fourth assault on Bhartpur the 76th Regiment

had 11 killed and 122 wounded. With these losses the regiment was practically annihilated as a fighting force. It lost altogether 44 killed and 260 wounded at Bhartpur; and during the entire campaign it had 15 officers and 155 non-commissioned officers and men killed, and 21 officers and 654 of other ranks wounded—a total of 36 officers and 809 men, which does not include deaths from disease. The wreck of the 76th went home shortly afterwards, with hardly an unwounded man in the ranks, and only two survivors of the original soldiers who had sailed for India under its colours.

The flank companies of the 22nd Regiment, which, as we have seen, served only during the latter portion of Lake's campaigns, also suffered very heavily. All the officers of the two companies, 4 in number, were severely wounded; and, of the rank and file, 27 were killed and 127 wounded—158 casualties in all. Such was active service in the days when the Indian Empire was a-making. Sergeant Shipp was immediately rewarded for his remarkable gallantry by a commission as ensign in the 65th Regiment, and very shortly afterwards he was promoted to a lieutenancy in the 76th.

After the failure of the fourth assault it was evident that no more could be attempted at Bhartpur until fresh supplies of food and ammunition had been collected, for both were practically exhausted. Lake, however, had no intention of removing his pressure from the fortress. On the night of February 22 the ordnance was withdrawn from the batteries, and on the 24th the army changed ground to a spot 6½ miles north-east of the town, covering the roads to Agra, Muttra, and Dig. Detachments were sent away for supplies, and the troops remaining in camp were set to work on the construction of great numbers of fascines and gabions. Fresh guns, with ammunition, were brought up from Fatehgarh and Aligarh, and those rendered unserviceable by constant firing were repaired.

The Raja of Bhartpur saw with alarm the determined attitude of Lake. His allies were rapidly failing him, his townspeople were beginning to lose heart, and he thought it was time to see what terms he could obtain.

The elevation of General Lake to the peerage afforded an opportunity of correspondence which the Raja eagerly seized, and, much to the amusement of the British army, a letter arrived from him on March 10 congratulating the Commander-in-Chief on his new honours, and intimating the Raja's desire to visit him in the British camp.

Whatever wish Lake may—nay, must—have felt to retrieve his failure, he was yet more anxious, for Lord Wellesley's sake, to bring the war to a close. This was clearly his first duty, so he at once entered into negotiations with the Raja.

While the terms of peace were under consideration, Major-General Smith arrived (on March 23) from his pursuit of Amir Khan. Lord Lake gave the cavalry a few days' rest, and then, about one in the morning of March 29, marched at their head silently out of camp, with the intention of beating up Holkar's headquarters, which lay about eight miles west of Bhartpur. The sound of the British guns was unfortunately heard, and Holkar escaped, losing in the pursuit, which extended over several miles, about 200 men, together with some elephants, camels, horses, and his camp.

Holkar then removed to a considerable distance southwest of Bhartpur, where he thought himself secure; but on April 2 Lord Lake made a similar night march with greater success, guided by Holkar's camp-fires alone. Heavy loss was inflicted on Holkar's troops, who dispersed in confusion. The British force sustained few casualties, but Holkar's losses were estimated at 1000 killed, and his scattered and demoralised troops were pursued for many miles over very broken ground. In this action the 27th and 29th Light Dragoons, like the Commander-in-Chief, appeared under new designations, having been respectively renumbered the 24th and 25th Light Dragoons.

On April 8 the army again changed its camp, marching to nearly the same place on the southeast of Bhartpur that it had occupied during the siege. This movement accelerated the conclusion of the treaty, the preliminaries of which were signed on April 10. Bhartpur remained in the possession of the Raja, but the fortress of Dig was to be kept in British hands until the Government should be satisfied as to the loyalty of the Raja, who pledged himself to hold no communication with the enemies of Great Britain, nor to employ any European in his service without the sanction of Government. The Raja also agreed to pay an indemnity of 20 *lakhs* of rupees (£200,000).

The British force before Bhartpur broke up on April 21, after lying there three months and twenty days.

It left behind it the dead bodies of a great number of brave soldiers and a considerable amount of prestige; for although the Jats and their Raja had been compelled to sue for peace, India long remembered that the great War Lord had sustained repeated defeats under the walls of Bhartpur, and had been unable in the end to effect its capture.

Raja Ranjit Singh died eight months after the repulse of Lake's last assault. In December 1825 Bhartpur was again besieged by a British army, under Lord Combermere, in consequence of the usurpation of the throne by a cousin of the recognised heir. Lord Combermere, though provided with a powerful artillery, found it impossible to breach the walls of Bhartpur, and the place was eventually captured by means of an immense mine. Lake, it is true, from the utter inadequacy of his means, did not succeed in his attempt; yet few soldiers will fail to recognise that his dogged persistence and his vigorous offensive action against the enemies in his rear, while incessantly assailing Bhartpur with the scanty resources at his disposal, offer a shining instance of determination such as has rarely been excelled.

CHAPTER 5

The End of the War

A passing reference was made in the preceding chapter to the elevation of General Lake to the peerage. The honour, as is shown by the title chosen, Lord Lake of Delhi and Laswari and of Aston Clinton, was granted as a reward for the campaign of 1803; but by the irony of fate, and thanks to the habitual delay of the British Government in conferring rewards, Lord Wellesley's letter informing Lake of his elevation did not reach him until March 8, 1805, when he was smarting from his final failure at Bhartpur, and we may be sure that so ill-timed a recompense lost much of its value to the recipient. Lord Lake was, however, as his reply to Lord Wellesley shows, grateful to the King who had sanctioned the reward, and to the Governor-General who had recommended it:

> Be assured that I feel much more than words can express for your kindness upon this and upon every other occasion, and would write more upon the subject was not my mind and time so much occupied with a variety of important objects, which I flatter myself will be found productive of the desired effect. I most sincerely lament our late disasters, which I own takes off much from the pleasure I should have received from the honours granted to me, but I trust before long to say I am in possession of this town.

Lord Lake, as we have seen, was destined never to possess Bhartpur, but he was too good a soldier, and too true to his duty, to allow this bitter blow to his pride to divert him from the main object in view—the termination of the war. The Raja of Bhartpur having ceased to be an active enemy, the obvious task before Lake was the extinction of Holkar, now the more pressing in that Sindhia was again showing signs of activity, and was evidently inclined to revive the Maratha Confederacy.

The forts and armies of Bhartpur no longer affording Holkar a base for operations against the Company's territories, he retired westward after Lord Lake's raid on April 2 and crossed the Chambal. The immense host with which Holkar had begun the campaign of 1804 was now reduced to 13,000 men, with between 20 and 30 worn-out guns; and although Lord Lake presently followed him, marching from Bhartpur on April 21, he did so more because of the necessity of checking the designs of Sindhia than with any hope of crushing the fugitive and swift-footed hordes of Holkar.

The threatened hostility of Sindhia hardly requires explanation. He was naturally ready to take the first opportunity of revenging himself for the events of 1803, and the failure of the first assault on Bhartpur appeared to him to mark the turn of the tide of British conquest.

Sindhia knew that Lake's victories had all been won, by a sort of miracle, with inadequate means. Such miracles, he thought, would no longer come to pass now that the spell of victory was broken; so Sindhia took heart of grace, and after the repulse of the first assault wrote to the Raja of Bhartpur urging him to hold out stoutly, promising to come to his assistance, and sounded Holkar as to the renewal of the confederation. Sindhia's letter fell into the hands of Lord Lake, who directed Mr Richard Jenkins, the acting Resident at Sindhia's Court, to retire thence and enter British territory. Sindhia, defiant though still undecided, refused to allow the departure of Mr Jenkins, and connived at the pillage of his camp-equipage and baggage.

On hearing of this incident Lake at once threatened Sindhia with hostilities, and the latter, although he eventually permitted Mr Jenkins to depart, retired to Kotah, attended by a number of Maratha and Rajput chiefs whom he had drawn from their allegiance to the British Government.

Lord Lake followed Sindhia as far as Dholpur, and having called the troops in Bundelkhand to join him, found himself by the end of April at the head of 18,000 men. Alarmed at this show of strength, many of Sindhia's adherents deserted him and proceeded, with their contingents, to Lake's headquarters, swelling his army to the imposing strength of 30,000 men. With camp-followers there were, writes Thorn, an aggregate of 300,000 people assembled on the barren rocks and sandbanks of the Chambal.

The defection of the chiefs from Sindhia and the disputes between him and Holkar having put an end to all immediate danger, Lord Lake determined to disperse this great assemblage, who could not long be maintained in so arid a region. On May 10, accordingly, the Bombay division marched for Rampura, and ten days later the Bundelkhand troops set out for their own province. There was, however, to be no repetition of the mistake of the previous year.

The Bengal army was all to remain, during the hot weather, west of the Jumna, and ready for prompt concentration should the necessity arise. Setting out from Dholpur on May 26, the troops were all cantoned early in June—the British infantry, under Colonel Monson, at Fatehpur Sikri; the artillery and the native cavalry and infantry divided between Agra and Muttra; while the three Light Dragoon regiments, with their galloper guns, housed themselves in the magnificent tomb of the Emperor Akbar at Sikandra and in the surrounding buildings.

The firm attitude of Lord Lake, supported as he was by the Governor-General, had had its inevitable effect on Sindhia, and there was every prospect of affairs between him and the British Government arriving at a satisfactory settlement. With this end in view Lord Wellesley was indeed prepared to make considerable concessions, but an event presently occurred which came near frustrating Lake's negotiations. This was the recall of Lord Wellesley from India and the appointment of Lord Cornwallis as his successor, pledged to a policy of peace and retrenchment. As far back as January 1802 Wellesley had informed the Court of Directors of his intention to resign the government of India, and he repeated this request in March of the same year.

The Directors, hesitating between a desire to recall a Governor-General who habitually disregarded their ideas and followed his own, and a feeling that it would be impossible to replace him, begged Wellesley to remain in office until January 1804. In accordance with his demand, this application of the Directors was warmly supported by the Ministry, and Wellesley consented to remain in office. Again in 1803 he desired to resign, and again he was requested to remain. This singular state of affairs continued, and when the home Government rewarded Lake and Arthur Wellesley for their services in the campaign of that year, Lord Wellesley not only received no reward but was practically censured by the Directors, who, while congratulating him on the brilliant successes of the campaign, declared that "they did not enter at present into the origin or policy of the war."

Thus although his sense of duty kept Wellesley from

again resigning his post while the difficulties brought about by his policy still existed, he expressed in the strongest language his hatred—for it was nothing less—of his masters in London. As he wrote to Castlereagh:

> Your lordship may be assured that as no symptom of tardy remorse displayed by the honourable Court in consequence of my recent successes will vary my present estimation of the faith and honour of my very worthy and approved good masters, or protract my continuance in India for one hour beyond the limits prescribed by the public interests, so no additional outrage, injury, or insult which can issue from the most loathsome den of the India House will accelerate my departure when the public safety shall appear to require my aid in this most arduous situation.

So Wellesley remained in office until the disaster to Monson's force gave the denizens of the said loathsome den an opportunity which they eagerly seized. Wellesley was recalled, and Lord Cornwallis having arrived at Calcutta on July 30, 1805, the great proconsul sailed on August 15 for England. His farewell letter to Lake shows his undiminished friendship, and his wish that Lake should not leave India until his work had been accomplished:

Fort William
July 30, 1805
My dear Lord,—The preparations for my approaching departure have occupied me so severely that I have been unable to reply to your last very kind and affectionate letters. This morning I have, to my very great satisfaction, been relieved from the charge of this Government by Lord Cornwallis; and I shall now be at liberty to answer your lordship's obliging private communications in the fullest manner, previously to

my actual embarkation. But I could not allow this express to depart without renewing to your lordship, in the most cordial spirit of gratitude, affection, and respect, the assurances of my unalterable friendship and attachment. I propose to embark between the 15th and 20th of August. Lord Cornwallis having written to your lordship, you will be apprised of the intentions of this Government respecting the state of affairs in Hindustan. You will also have learnt the arrangements which have been made in England with regard to your own situation. On this subject I shall offer no further remark than that my wish must be to preserve your lordship's invaluable services until affairs shall have been finally settled in India. As far as your kindness to me is concerned, your lordship will best satisfy my mind by continuing to serve your country in this quarter of the globe to the completion of every object of peace and prosperity. Lord Cornwallis will probably embark on the river before I can attempt to sail in the present state of the season. It is doubtful whether any letter from your lordship, however, would now find me in India; but I sincerely hope to hear from you fully and frequently in England.

Ever, my dear lord, yours most sincerely and affectionately,

Wellesley

In accordance with his promise to the Directors, Lord Cornwallis immediately set about the task of reducing expenditure, and on his first working day in India wrote thus to Lake: "It is my earnest desire, if it should be possible, to put an end to this most unprofitable and ruinous warfare."

The voice of history has declared that Lord Wellesley's wars were neither unprofitable nor ruinous. On the contrary, they averted ruin and established an Empire; but the dying eyes of Cornwallis could not see the truth. Soon, indeed, they saw no more in this world, for having set out from Calcutta for Allahabad, in order to provide personally that his measures should be carried into execution, Lord Cornwallis died at Ghazipur on October 5, 1805.

Much as we must deplore the orders which the dying Governor-General sent to Lake, which, but for the firmness of the latter, would in all probability have caused the dying war again to spring to life, no reproachful words shall here be written of one who had been in his day a clear-sighted statesman and an able soldier, and was always an upright English gentleman.

The instructions sent by Cornwallis to Lake, dated September 19, were to the following effect. All points under dispute with Sindhia were to be surrendered; Gohad and Gwalior were to be returned; Delhi was to be abandoned; and Sindhia was to be permitted to restore Maratha influence in Hindustan; the Company's border was to be drawn back from the Chambal to the Jumna; and British protection was to be withdrawn from the native princes whose territories lay between these rivers. Dholpur was to be given back to Sindhia, and the Raja of Jaipur was to be left to make terms for himself as best he could.

In sending this letter to Lord Lake, the Governor-General enclosed one for Sindhia to the same effect.

The terms proposed being a complete surrender of the conquests made during the war, which was still unfinished, the letter was nothing less than a confession of defeat, and would undoubtedly have been so regarded by Sindhia and every ruling prince in India. The proposal to abandon to their enemies the chiefs with whom alliances had been concluded, ranks with the most humiliating and dishonouring policies ever imposed on an English general by his employers.

To his eternal honour, Lord Lake took all risks and detained the letter to Sindhia, pending a reply to the remonstrance which he addressed to Lord Cornwallis. Before it could reach him the Governor-General was dead. He was succeeded by Sir George Barlow, the senior member of Council, who had held a dormant commission during the Governor-Generalship of Lord Wellesley. Barlow's opinions at this time reflected those of Lord Cornwallis, just as they had reflected those of Wellesley while the latter was in office. As a civil servant of the Company, Barlow was indeed in duty bound, when a free agent, to carry out what he knew to be the wishes of the Court of Directors, and the death of Lord Cornwallis, therefore, did little to diminish the difficulties of Lake in his negotiations with Sindhia.

That Lake was able to carry them eventually to a successful issue is partly due to the happy circumstance that Colonel (afterwards Sir John) Malcolm was now his political assistant. Malcolm was entirely in sympathy with "the forward policy" of Wellesley and Lake, but was able from his position and training to calm the anxiety of Sir George Barlow, and so gain the time necessary to complete the bargain with Sindhia. A treaty fixing the British border at the Chambal was finally accepted by Sindhia in November, but a month earlier Lake's mind was so far at rest that he had been able to set out from Muttra to deal once and for all with Holkar.

Reference has been made to the rupture between Holkar and Sindhia, after which incident the former, attended by Amir Khan, had proceeded to Ajmir. After vainly endeavouring to persuade the Raja of Jaipur to join him, Holkar marched northward in September, hoping to obtain the support of the chiefs of the southern Sikh states, of whom the most powerful were the Rajas of Patiala, Nabha, and Jhind. Holkar marched through Shekawatti, skirting Alwar and Rewari, to Dadri in Jhajhar, where he left his infantry, numbering about 3000, with 1000 cavalry and 30 guns, to harry the British territories. He himself, with about 11,000 horse, went on to Patiala.

Lord Lake immediately pursued him, marching from Muttra towards Delhi on October 10, and disposing the bulk of his troops for the protection of the northern portion of the Doab, both against Holkar's infantry and any attack that the Sikh chiefs might be induced to make. These dispositions proved effectual, and we need only follow the march of the small body of troops with which Lord Lake personally pursued Holkar. This consisted of two brigades of cavalry, composed of the three Light Dragoon regiments and the 3rd and 5th Bengal Cavalry, Captain Brown's battery of Horse Artillery, some field-guns, and the reserve infantry brigade, now composed of the entire 22nd Regiment, the Bengal European Regiment, the 1st Battalion 9th and the 1st Battalion 11th Native Infantry. Colonel Need commanded the 1st Brigade of Cavalry, and with the tough old Commander-in-Chief was one of the few senior officers remaining with the army who had taken the field at the beginning of the war.

On October 28 Lake's force met on the march the garrison of Dig, that fortress having been returned to the Raja of Bhartpur in consideration of a large money payment, which supplied Lake's army with the sinews of war. Lake arrived at Delhi on November 7, and was at Panipat, the famous battlefield on which the mastery of India had so often been decided, on November 17. Here Lake picked up the column, under Colonel Burn, which had been cantoned at Panipat during the hot weather. Burn's force included Skinner's horse, and with his force thus considerably increased, Lord Lake confidently followed Holkar. There was still a chance that Ranjit Singh, now the most powerful of the Sikh chiefs north of the Sutlej, might assist the fugitive, but Lake was for the moment free of control from Calcutta;

he had money enough for present needs in his treasury, a sufficient force at his disposal, and he was determined to bring the war to a decisive issue.

On November 24 the British force arrived at Patiala, where the Raja informed Lake that he had refused to assist Holkar with men or money. The southern Sikh states had indeed decided to accept British protection, in preference to absorption by the growing power of Ranjit Singh.

The pursuit of Holkar still continued, and on December 2 the army arrived at Ludhiana, a town standing on a tributary of the river Sutlej, the southern boundary of the Punjab. Holkar had already crossed the river and was at Jalandhar, some thirty miles farther north. Lord Lake was now anxious to make a forward dash, and, if possible, bring Holkar to a decisive action; but the native regiments showed considerable reluctance to cross the Sutlej, probably on account of some religious prejudice. Here the unquestioning loyalty of Skinner's horse proved of great service.

Knowing that Skinner would undertake any task, and that his men would follow him blindfold, Lord Lake, when at dinner on December 3, observed that he wished someone would try the ford over the Sutlej with a troop and a galloper gun. To leave no room for a mistake, Colonel Worsley, the Adjutant-General, told Skinner that the hint was intended for him. Skinner writes in his memoirs:

> On which I immediately rose and said, 'If your lordship will give me leave, I will try the ford tomorrow morning.' He replied, 'Be there about dawn with two rissalahs of your yellow boys and a galloper, and I will also be with you.

Skinner continues that on the following morning he crossed the Sutlej, though with some difficulty, his horses

having to swim for about twenty yards, and the gun sticking in a quicksand. However, in less than an hour they
were all well over, and Skinner took off his hat and gave
three cheers, in which Lord Lake, Malcolm, and the staff all
heartily joined, proclaiming that the first British gun had
entered the Punjab.

Meanwhile Malcolm, with his usual tact and knowledge
of the native character, had pointed out to the sepoys that
there could be no objection to crossing over towards Amritsar, a sacred Hindu city. They were at once persuaded,
and made no difficulty when a battalion was ordered to
cross and secure the ford on December 5. On the following day the whole army crossed the Sutlej, and on the 7th
marched on towards the Bias, the northern tributary of that
river. On December 8 Skinner was sent on with 400 of his
men to find Holkar. After a march of thirty miles Skinner
came to the south bank of the Bias, to find that Holkar
had crossed the river. His rear-guard were still on the north
bank, and fired a few rounds from an 18 -pounder at Skinner's men. These were the last shots of the war.

Holkar was now at Amritsar, but could fly no farther,
as Ranjit Singh refused to befriend him. During Lake's
march through the southern Punjab the utmost care had
been taken to give no offence to the population, the troops
maintaining strict discipline and paying liberally for all
supplies. Still, Ranjit Singh was desirous that Lake's army
should penetrate no farther into the Sikh country, and it
was clearly a time for patience and diplomacy.

Lake and his army therefore encamped on the south
bank of the Bias opposite Amritsar, and Charles Metcalfe
was deputed to enter into negotiations with Holkar. This
proved a most difficult task for the young diplomatist, for
Holkar, in spite of the difficulties of his own position, was
ready to presume on the pacific spirit that he knew actu-

ated the British Government. Metcalfe, however, young as he was, had the necessary strength of character to play a firm part. He and Colonel Malcolm were politicians of the Wellesley school, and being aware that the new Cornwallis-Barlow policy of flabby surrender would merely defeat its own ends and fail to secure peace, they heartily encouraged Lord Lake in the line of action congenial to him.

Lake showed himself, as ever, strong and bold. A long career, ending in four strenuous years of Indian warfare, had sapped his constitution, but he still appeared to possess his full vigour of body, and no weakness of will had overtaken him. Ignoring all timid instructions from Calcutta, he refused to make further concessions, and finally declared that if the treaty as propounded by Metcalfe were not signed within three days, he would cross the Bias and march upon Holkar's camp.

Metcalfe has left in a private letter an interesting account of his negotiations with *Ek-chasm-ud-daula* ("His one-eyed Highness," as it may be translated). He describes Holkar's appearance as:

> . . . . very grave, his countenance expressive, his manners and conversation easy. He has not at all the appearance of the savage we know him to be. . . . A little lap-dog was on his *musnud*, a strange playfellow for Holkar. The jewels on his neck were invaluably rich.

Holkar was still attended by Amir Khan, whom Metcalfe describes as:

> . . . . blackguard in his looks. . . . He affected on the occasion of my reception to be particularly fierce, by rubbing his coat over with gunpowder and assuming in every way the air of a common soldier.

Lord Lake's firmness, and the conviction that he would make good his threat to attack, brought Holkar to his knees. His troops had no more fight in them, and the Sikhs, not yet welded into a nation by Ranjit Singh, could not help even had they desired to do so; so on January 7, 1803, a treaty of peace was signed between Holkar and the British Government, and the long-drawn-out war was at last at an end.

The terms, as usual, were generous. Large possessions were restored to the man who, a little time before, had declared that he could carry his all on his saddle. Holkar was required to renounce all claims on the territory north of the Chambal and in Bundelkhand, and, like Sindhia, to engage to employ no Europeans without the consent of the British Government; he was to relinquish his claims on Rampura and against the Raja of Bundi, and to return to his own territories by a route prescribed, with the intention of keeping his ill-disciplined army from molesting the chiefs who had befriended the English during the war. On the other hand, Holkar received back all the territory south of the Tapti and Godaveri rivers that had been captured from him during the war, and he was confirmed in the possession of his provinces south of the Chambal. He was, in fact, restored to his original position, losing his temporary acquisitions, but deprived of nothing.

Such a conclusion to the war was both satisfactory and honourable, and Lord Lake had fair reason to suppose that Sir George Barlow would accept the settlement. When announcing to him the signature of the treaty, Lake writes:

I offer my most cordial congratulations on an event which promises to restore complete tranquillity to India, and which you, I am satisfied, will judge to be highly favourable to the interests of the British Government.

Sir George Barlow, however, was not content. He was bent on a retrograde policy, and on repudiating all protective obligations. Therefore, in ratifying Lake's treaties with

Sindhia and Holkar, Barlow added to them certain "declaratory" articles, which practically abandoned the small states west of the Jumna to the vengeance of the Marathas.

Sir George Barlow is perhaps not to be judged by the same standard as an ordinary Governor-General. He was not, like Wellesley, a great nobleman, an Imperial statesman, governing India for its own good, but also for the advantage of the Empire. Barlow was merely a servant of the East India Company, pledged, as he believed, to carry out the timid and huckstering policy of Leadenhall Street, and the onus of his base surrender of the allies of England rests perhaps chiefly on the Directors rather than on him.

Whosoever the blame, Lord Lake would no more consent to exercise political duties, nor to connive at the abandonment of faithful friends. He had already suffered sufficient humiliation from the repudiation by Lord Cornwallis of his engagements to the corps of irregulars.

Sir George Barlow's abandonment of the Rajput chief was the last straw. Lake therefore resigned his political functions, and prepared to retain his office of Commander-in-Chief only until he should have been able to carry out the task of demobilising the army and placing it in its peace stations. His conduct at this juncture is thus described by Metcalfe,—a civil servant, be it remembered,—in a letter dated February 12, 1806:

> Lord Lake has acted in a dignified and noble manner. He declares his sentiments in opposition to those of the Governor-General, and he urges every argument and fact which he hopes will induce him to alter his plans. Having done this, he is determined not to embarrass or counteract the views of the Government; and feeling that he cannot be a fit instrument for the execution of measures which he entirely dis-

approves. . . . his lordship is resolved to resign all political powers and to confine his attention to military
arrangements. His despatches are marked equally by
proper respect and manly firmness.

Lord Lake's army commenced its return march to Hindustan on January 9, two days after the acceptance of the
treaty by Holkar, and re-crossed the Sutlej on January 18.
The march was subsequently continued in a leisurely manner, delay being caused by late winter rains.

At Karnal, reached on February 10, a detachment of two
battalions of sepoys, with Skinner's horse, was left in garrison under Brigadier-General Burn, the remainder of the
army, with the Commander-in-Chief, arriving at Delhi on
February 15.

Lord Lake remained two months at Delhi, and was
obliged to keep the army in readiness for action by the
unsatisfactory conduct of Holkar, who showed great dis-
inclination to return to his own dominions and a fixed intention of maltreating the Rajput states. Sir George Barlow
was, however, no less fixed in his policy of non-interven-
tion, and Lord Lake had to endure the humiliation of being
reproached by the Raja of Jaipur for his impending ruin.

While at Delhi several fetes were given to the army, the
most magnificent being that given by the Begum Sumru, a
lady who, though, as Thorn mentions, "somewhat advanced
in years," took great delight in camp life, and was a warm
admirer of Lord Lake and his army.

Having completed all the necessary arrangements for
the distribution of the troops, Lord Lake went on his way
to Cawnpore, and thence to Calcutta. In February 1807 he
embarked for England, "followed," writes Thorn, "by the
prayers of the people of India, as well natives as Europeans,
who esteemed him for his personal virtues no less than they
admired him for his unshaken firmness in war, the vigour

of his operations, the judgment displayed in his plans, and the liberality of his conduct in the hour of victory."

Lord Lake was one of the most popular Commanders-in-Chief who ever served in India; yet he was a strict disciplinarian, and he never spared his troops when there was an attack to be made or hard marching to be undertaken. He lived before the growth of the strange theory that victories could be won and armies defeated without loss of life, so the soldiers who served him knew that he would call upon them to face hardship, wounds, and death. Yet they served Lake willingly, for they always saw him share with them the toil and the danger, and they knew by a hundred proofs that he was generous and kind-hearted.

No one was more closely associated with Lake in the last portion of his arduous Indian career than Colonel, afterwards Sir John, Malcolm, and no one was better fitted than he to judge of the quality and character of a man. His picture of Lake, from a private letter, is therefore of special value.

> I am truly proud to think that I have succeeded, to the very extent of my hope, in obtaining Lord Lake's uniform approbation; and you will be surprised to learn that I have had the good fortune to go on, through the arduous and vexatious scene in which I have been engaged, without once displeasing his lordship in the most trifling instance. And, indeed, I have every hour received, from the first day I joined to the present moment, fresh marks of his regard, esteem, and confidence, which I attribute in the first instance to the respect and affection which Lord Lake entertains for Lord Wellesley, and the inclination he in consequence feels to be kind to any person honoured by his protection; and, in the second, to the direct course I have observed, and the freedom with

which I have expressed my sentiments on every occasion. For, believe me, whatever defects there may be in the character of Lord Lake (and he, like other men, has his share), that of want of accurate observation of those about him is not of the number. Indeed, he appreciates, as justly as any man I ever knew in my life, the characters and views of those with whom he has personal communication.

As for myself, I have a sincere attachment to the old lord, which has been created by a full knowledge of his many admirable qualities. His heart is kind almost to weakness. He is honourable in the fullest sense of the word. As to his military talents, let his life speak. Without that regular system, and without that comprehensive mind which theorists may conclude indispensable to form a great leader, he will (as far as I can judge), from his attention to the temper and character of those he commands—from his looking, in military points, to essentials and not trifles— and from his extraordinary energy, courage, and animation, always do more with troops than those who may be reputed abler; and I am satisfied that he will always merit and enjoy the highest confidence of those under his orders. I thought you would be anxious to know what I thought of Lord Lake, and I have told you sincerely. Many may differ; but I have formed my opinion after a good deal of reflection, and after having had the best opportunity of judging of most parts of his character.

This very interesting study gives the clue to much of Lord Lake's extraordinary power of commanding the confidence of his officers and men, that quality the absence of which nullifies all the other talents of a general. It was because his army saw that Lake looked to essentials and not to trifles that they believed in him, and it was his energy, courage, animation, and sympathy that gave him the magnetic influence over his soldiers of all races that carried him so often to victory in the face of difficulties and odds that seemed overpowering.

If these great qualities earned for Lake the veneration of his army, as indeed they did, his very foibles and habits were such as pleased the soldiers of his day. Sir John Kaye writes:

> He had no small contempt for civilians and penmen. 'Damn your writing—mind your fighting,' was the exhortation which he blurted out in the rude language of the camp. He was a disciplinarian and something of a formalist. It mattered not at what time of the morning the army commenced its march, there was Lord Lake in full uniform, buttoned to the chin, powdered, and peruked. But there was a warm heart beneath the rigid exterior, and no man was more beloved by all ranks of the army.

There is an honourable confirmation of this last statement in Lieut.-Colonel Innes's ' History of the Bengal European Regiment, Lord Lake's own "Dirty Shirts":

> He was beloved by the Bengal European Regiment. The anniversary of his death was for many years observed with solemnity, and his memory was at all times held dear by those officers who had had the glorious privilege of serving under him in the field.

Such was the feeling towards Lord Lake of those who served England under his command. A record of the estimation in which he was held by the great Governor - General, to whom he devoted every faculty of mind and body from the day of his arrival in India, addressed to the Prince of Wales it has happily been preserved, and with it we may fitly conclude this estimate of Lake's quality as a soldier.

I am anxious to offer my congratulations to your Royal Highness upon the brilliant and highly useful services of General Lake. His masterly operations, his unexampled alacrity and honourable zeal, the judgment, skill, and promptitude of decision which he has manifested in every crisis of difficulty or danger, combined with his irresistible spirit of enterprise and courage, entitle him to the gratitude and admiration of every loyal British subject, and of every heart and mind which can feel for the honour, or can understand the interests, of the British Empire.

It is strange but true that the object of this eulogium from the illustrious Wellesley has been forgotten by his countrymen, or remembered, if at all, rather by his failure to capture Bhartpur than by his long life of faithful and loyal service, and by the glorious victories of his Indian campaigns.

The remainder of Lord Lake's story may be dismissed in a few words. Having completed his period of service as Commander-in-Chief in India, he embarked for home in February 1807. In October of the same year he was raised to the rank of Viscount, but survived this new honour but a few months.

In February 1808, while serving as president of the court-martial on the unfortunate General Whitelocke, Lord Lake suddenly fell ill, in consequence of a violent chill aggravated, according to a family tradition, by the refusal of the punctilious old soldier to wear a greatcoat. His constitution, sapped by long and arduous service, gave way, and after three days of suffering, he died on February 20, 1808, at the age of sixty-three years. Lake's last day on earth was cheered by the kindness of his old master and friend, the Prince Regent, who paid him a long visit, and was seen to be in tears as he left the dying man.

Just a hundred years have elapsed since death put a period to Lake's long and faithful services to England. In that he did not escape calumny he but shared the fate of every soldier, seaman, and statesman who has held high office in our party-swayed country. The slanders which assailed Lake, in common with all who had borne a part in the conquests of Wellesley, were easily and promptly disproved. It was readily shown that with great opportunities of blamelessly acquiring wealth, Lake had died a poor man, leaving but a pittance to his family. Time, however, while clearing his honour, has robbed Lake of an inheritance to which he was entitled, the fame of a commander who never encountered defeat in the field. Malleson, in a striking passage, compared Lake with Clive for his calmness of mind and clearness of vision in the stress and turmoil of battle; and for this rare and priceless quality, and for his commanding influence in moments when victory and defeat were hanging in the balance, Lake will bear comparison with an even greater commander.

In the battles of the future the personal influence of the commander, though differently manifested, will still be decisive. No longer will it be possible for him, like Lake at Laswari or Wellesley at Assaye, to lead in the charge both his cavalry and his infantry, and to watch with his own eyes every shifting-phase of the battle. Yet the same qualities that gave Lake his long train of victories at Aligarh, Delhi, Agra, and Laswari, that encouraged him to deal blow after blow at Bhartpur, regardless of the hosts that encompassed his small army, the qualities of daring enterprise and iron determination, will alone secure success in future wars as they have in the past.

Commanders of the type of Lake may make mistakes, but they win victories, and their value to the countries that give them birth is inestimable.

LEONAUR

ALSO FROM LEONAUR
AVAILABLE IN SOFTCOVER OR HARDCOVER WITH DUST JACKET

THE COMPLEAT RIFLEMAN HARRIS by Benjamin Harris as told to & transcribed by Captain Henry Curling—The adventures of a soldier of the 95th (Rifles) during the Peninsular Campaign of the Napoleonic Wars

WITH WELLINGTON'S LIGHT CAVALRY by William Tomkinson—The Experiences of an officer of the 16th Light Dragoons in the Peninsular and Waterloo campaigns of the Napoleonic Wars.

SERGEANT BOURGOGNE by Adrien Bourgogne—With Napoleon's Imperial Guard in the Russian Campaign and on the Retreat from Moscow 1812 - 13.

SWORDS OF HONOUR by Henry Newbolt & Stanley L. Wood—The Careers of Six Outstanding Officers from the Napoleonic Wars, the Wars for India and the American Civil War, with dozens of illustrations by Stanley L. Wood.

SURTEES OF THE RIFLES by William Surtees—A Soldier of the 95th (Rifles) in the Peninsular campaign of the Napoleonic Wars.

ENSIGN BELL IN THE PENINSULAR WAR by George Bell—The Experiences of a young British Soldier of the 34th Regiment 'The Cumberland Gentlemen' in the Napoleonic wars.

HUSSAR IN WINTER by Alexander Gordon—A British Cavalry Officer during the retreat to Corunna in the Peninsular campaign of the Napoleonic Wars.

NAPOLEONIC WAR STORIES by Sir Arthur Quiller-Couch—Tales of soldiers, spies, battles & sieges from the Peninsular & Waterloo campaingns.

JOURNALS OF ROBERT ROGERS OF THE RANGERS by Robert Rogers—The exploits of Rogers & the Rangers in his own words during 1755-1761 in the French & Indian War.

KERSHAW'S BRIGADE VOLUME 1 by D. Augustus Dickert—Manassas, Seven Pines, Sharpsburg (Antietam), Fredricksburg, Chancellorsville, Gettysburg, Chickamauga, Chattanooga, Fort Sanders & Bean Station..

KERSHAW'S BRIGADE VOLUME 2 by D. Augustus Dickert—At the wilderness, Cold Harbour, Petersburg, The Shenandoah Valley and Cedar Creek.

A TIGER ON HORSEBACK by L. March Phillips—The Experiences of a Trooper & Officer of Rimington's Guides - The Tigers - during the Anglo-Boer war 1899 - 1902.

LEONAUR

ALSO FROM LEONAUR
AVAILABLE IN SOFTCOVER OR HARDCOVER WITH DUST JACKET

EW2 EYEWITNESS TO WAR SERIES
CAPTAIN OF THE 95th (Rifles) by Jonathan Leach

An officer of Wellington's Sharpshooters during the
Peninsular, South of France and Waterloo Campaigns
of the Napoleonic Wars.

SOFTCOVER : **ISBN 1-84677-001-7**
HARDCOVER : **ISBN 1-84677-016-5**

WFI THE WARFARE FICTION SERIES
NAPOLEONIC WAR STORIES
by Sir Arthur Quiller-Couch

Tales of soldiers, spies, battles & Sieges from the
Peninsular & Waterloo campaigns

SOFTCOVER : **ISBN 1-84677-003-3**
HARDCOVER : **ISBN 1-84677-014-9**

EWI EYEWITNESS TO WAR SERIES
RIFLEMAN COSTELLO by Edward Costello

The adventures of a soldier of the 95th (Rifles) in the
Peninsular & Waterloo Campaigns of the Napoleonic wars.

SOFTCOVER : **ISBN 1-84677-000-9**
HARDCOVER : **ISBN 1-84677-018-1**

MCI THE MILITARY COMMANDERS SERIES
JOURNALS OF ROBERT ROGERS OF THE RANGERS by Robert Rogers

The exploits of Rogers & the Rangers in his own words
during 1755-1761 in the French & Indian War.

SOFTCOVER : **ISBN 1-84677-002-5**
HARDCOVER : **ISBN 1-84677-010-6**

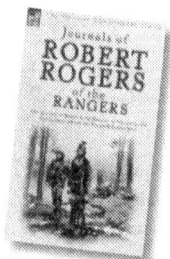

www.ingramcontent.com/pod-product-compliance
Lightning Source LLC
Chambersburg PA
CBHW020244290326
41930CB00038B/313